BUILDING DISTINCTIVE BRAND ASSETS

BUILDING
DISTINCTIVE
BRAND
ASSETS

JENNI ROMANIUK

OXFORD
UNIVERSITY PRESS
AUSTRALIA & NEW ZEALAND

OXFORD
UNIVERSITY PRESS

Oxford University Press is a department of the University of Oxford.
It furthers the University's objective of excellence in research,
scholarship, and education by publishing worldwide. Oxford is a registered
trademark of Oxford University Press in the UK and in certain other
countries.

Published in Australia by
Oxford University Press
Level 8, 737 Bourke Street, Docklands, Victoria 3008, Australia

© Jenni Romaniuk 2018

The moral rights of the author have been asserted.

First published 2018
Reprinted 2018 (twice), 2022, 2023 (twice)

A catalogue record for this
book is available from the
National Library of Australia

Reproduction and communication for educational purposes
The Australian *Copyright Act 1968* (the Act) allows a maximum of one chapter
or 10% of the pages of this work, whichever is the greater, to be reproduced
and/or communicated by any educational institution for its educational purposes
provided that the educational institution (or the body that administers it) has
given a remuneration notice to Copyright Agency Limited (CAL) under the Act.

For details of the CAL licence for educational institutions contact:

Copyright Agency Limited
Level 15, 233 Castlereagh Street
Sydney NSW 2000
Telephone: (02) 9394 7600
Facsimile: (02) 9394 7601
Email: info@copyright.com.au

Edited by Susan Keogh, Apostrophes, Etc.
Typeset by Newgen KnowledgeWorks Pvt. Ltd., Chennai, India
Proofread by Natasha Broadstock
Printed in China by Sheck Wah Tong Printing Press Ltd.

Links to third party websites are provided by Oxford in good faith and for information only.
Oxford disclaims any responsibility for the materials contained in any third party website
referenced in this work.

CONTENTS

FIGURES AND TABLES

FIGURES

TABLES

ABOUT THE AUTHORS

Jenni Romaniuk is a Research Professor and Associate Director (International) at the Ehrenberg-Bass Institute. A pioneer in Distinctive Asset and Mental Availability strategy and measurement, her research expertise also includes brand health measurement, word-of-mouth and advertising effectiveness. She is also the lead author of *How Brands Grow Part 2* (Oxford University Press, 2016). Her passion for branding and improving the quality of advertising tends to ruin most co-viewing experiences.

Ella Ward is a Senior Marketing Scientist at the Ehrenberg-Bass Institute, University of South Australia. Her areas of research expertise are branding, identifying and combatting mental competition, identity design and management for brand portfolios, and Distinctive Asset measurement. As a total sugar addict, Ella has been known to use 'brand research' as an excuse for the various chocolate bars hidden in her desk drawer.

William Caruso is a Senior Marketing Scientist at the Ehrenberg-Bass Institute, at the University of South Australia. His research expertise covers shopper behaviour, in-store merchandising, eye-tracking, and physical availability to improve retailing performance. While Will is very committed to producing and disseminating knowledge about marketing, he is also a semi-professional race car driver nicknamed 'Will the Thrill', who can be found most weekends at speedway dirt tracks racing a very distinct number 10 wingless sprintcar.

ACKNOWLEDGMENTS

I'd like to thank my friends, family, colleagues who put up with my obsession with Distinctive Assets as I wrote *Building Distinctive Brand Assets*. Thank you for at least pretending to be as excited about this as I am. In particular, thanks to Will and Ella, my co-authors, who helped bring this to fruition; to Magda, for the unending enthusiasm that kept me motivated; and to Elke and Liz, who take care of the administrative stuff that gives me the freedom to concentrate on the things I do best. Thank you also to my office mates Alfie and Honey, who reminded me to get up and see the sun at least two times a day. Finally, thank you to my clients whose questions and discussions fuelled the issues raised in this research, and the Ehrenberg-Bass Institute's researchers and corporate sponsors who help to build a stronger, evidence-based marketing discipline.

INTRODUCTION

Building Distinctive Brand Assets is for anyone with a brand logo, font or colour scheme. It has particular relevance for those who have wondered if (or have been told) it's time for a change.

> Marketing has changed the logo again. How much is that going to cost?
> Don't these people have any serious work to do?
>
> Secret thought of a CFO

Despite advances in our understanding of how the brain, memory and buyer behaviour work, much of the advice on building a strong brand identity is tied up in folklore, pop psychology or based on out-of-date brand strategies. Books on the topic tend to see brand identity as a design exercise, with aesthetics at the core of choices, or inextricably tie brand identity with brand positioning, which is akin to stamping an expiry date on your branding efforts.

Somewhere, there is a sad graveyard filled with logos, characters, pack designs and taglines discarded as a result of misguided decisions. For marketing to be taken seriously as a discipline, we need rigorous evidence to underpin decisions around one of the most visible areas of brand management. My ambition for this book is that it reduces the number of public mistakes we make, such as resource-draining logo (Gap) or pack (Tropicana) changes that consumers don't need or want. These changes damage the brand and the credibility of marketers. I also hope this book helps marketers better utilise their brand's identity, and harness the value from underdeveloped and underleveraged assets.

Building Distinctive Brand Assets will help you set up a long-term strategy to build a strong brand identity. It explains the knowledge, metrics and management systems needed to build and protect strong assets.

This book is about building Distinctive Assets

The Oxford Dictionary definition gives two facets to being distinct.

dis·tinct

də'stiNG(k)t/

adjective: distinct

1. recognisably different in nature from something else of a similar type

2. readily distinguishable by the senses.

Both of these facets are important when thinking about Distinctive Assets, which are the non–brand name elements that trigger the brand into the memory of category buyers (Romaniuk, 2016b; Sharp & Romaniuk, 2010).

Distinctive Assets make up the brand's identity—how people sense it. These assets are a product of how the company has presented the brand to the world. But not all marketer actions effectively build Distinctive Assets. Only the actions that have fought through barriers of inattention and mental competition make a lasting impact on category buyers. In *Building Distinctive Brand Assets* you will learn how to overcome these barriers.

The insights in *Building Distinctive Brand Assets* are gathered from empirical research into the brain, memory, marketing and media. In addition, the new studies it includes further our understanding about how to develop Distinctive Assets.

Thank you to my clients and colleagues for their thoughtful questions. Much of the content and structure draws from these questions. Thank you also to the brands that have provided the examples in this book. For the marketers of brands I draw on to illustrate mistakes I see made, my apologies in advance if any offence is taken. My intent is to instruct rather than offend. Also be assured your brand is rarely alone in error, but simply chosen as the brand that was mentally available for that topic when I wrote that section. Therefore, in one way it is something of a compliment to be chosen, as it shows your brand's marketing activities have cut through to my very cluttered brain. And you get a free brand placement!

It's time to celebrate the act of branding

The art of branding is lauded, the science of branding is revered—but rarely is the actual *act* of branding celebrated. *Building Distinctive Brand Assets* is for people who want to get better at branding. If a runner wants to improve his or her time for a 200-metre sprint, he/she works to correct the important inputs, such as gait, diet and training regime. Top runners don't change everything but focus attention on the areas that matter. In a similar vein, by understanding the aspects most influential for building Distinctive Assets, you can improve your efforts. Here, I highlight the strategies and actions that work, as well as the ones that don't, to help you take advantage of opportunities, to evolve when needed and to anticipate, therefore avoiding, potential minefields.

Why you might hate this book (but should read it anyway)

Any book in the area of brand identity is going to come under criticism from a number of fronts. My discussions with marketers and agencies, as well as academic colleagues, have raised three points of potential contention that I want to directly address.

1 *Your rules take away the creative magic*: the art versus science debate becomes pronounced when treading into areas such as design. My aim is not to stifle creativity but to identify operational boundaries, so creativity can have the best opportunity to succeed. Don't shoot the messenger! I did not create these boundaries: they come from our brains, the environment and the actions of competitors. Ignoring them will not make them go away. *Building Distinctive Brand Assets* is based on the premise that the better we understand these challenges, the better we can address them.

2 *You don't provide enough clear instructions on what to do*: if you are looking for a paint-by-numbers approach to building a brand's identity, then you will be disappointed. I do provide some clear tactical guidelines but the aim is to equip you with the information to make evidence-based, informed decisions, not to make those decisions for you. No single path leads to a strong Distinctive Asset. Most of the effort is about setting forth on the right path and avoiding distractions. Not very glamorous I know, but neither is lithium. But lithium is very valuable, not because it makes something sparkly like diamonds, but because it is an essential component in something everyone needs: rechargeable batteries. The big, flashy, shiny thing gets all the attention, but much of an effective Distinctive Asset's strategy is rooted in the quiet, behind-the-scenes discipline of persisting on a path of consistent, excellent execution.

3 *This research doesn't apply in a disruptive, world of rapid change*: the curious thing about change is not that it happens, but humanity's capacity to stay constant when facing even the most disruptive changes. For example a study found that lottery winners, after a spike in happiness, quickly revert back to their pre-win happiness level (Brickman, Coates & Janoff-Bulman, 1978). When faced with new situations, our brain tends to adapt, rather than revolt. Our branding tactics do need to adapt to environmental change: for example specifically using Distinctive Assets that work better on a mobile phone rather than a one-size-fits-all branding strategy. The frameworks provided are designed to adapt to new contexts, even ones we can't yet anticipate. Good branding strategy is also largely about first asking the right questions. *Building Distinctive Brand Assets* gives you those questions.

What to expect

Building Distinctive Brand Assets is divided into three broad sections. The first section is about strategy, and answers the 'why build Distinctive Assets' question. It covers how Distinctive Assets are created and their role in a broader brand strategy. The second section is about measurement: the 'how strong are your brand's Distinctive Assets' question. It covers measurement approaches, metrics and how to use these metrics.

The third section deals with asset choice and implementation: the 'which assets to build' question. It covers types of assets, introduces the idea of a Distinctive Asset *palette* and examines different types of *visual* and *audio* assets including *celebrities*, *taglines* and *colour-based* assets. It also outlines how to set up a Distinctive Asset *management system* to manage and monitor a brand's assets and provide an early warning system to identify potential threats before they evolve into major issues.

The chapters are deliberately succinct: the reference list at the end provides a wealth of material for going deeper into each topic or you can reach out to me if you have particular questions. My desire was to make each topic easy to find and understand, so that you can use *Building Distinctive Brand Assets* as an ongoing reference guide as specific issues arise. You can reach me at jenni@marketingscience.info for any comments or questions, or message me on LinkedIn.

Jenni

1

The Seven Costly Sins of Brand Identity

JENNI ROMANIUK

In the words of the old adage, 'the road to hell is paved with good intentions'. While having a weak brand identity might not quite be equivalent to being in hell, there are still some actions, taken with the best of intent, that nonetheless diminish the value of Distinctive Assets. These seven costly sins summarise some of the common mistakes I have observed in my time researching Distinctive Assets and brand identity. Which might you by guilty of . . . ?

Pride

Pride, in brand identity, manifests when the brand's growth or decline in sales is attributed to its Distinctive Assets. Growth is purportedly driven by the new tagline, or signing of a particular celebrity, while decline is the fault of a stale or old-fashioned identity. Distinctive Assets, being visible to the wider public, become easy change targets when someone wants to send a signal to the wider market (customers, shareholders, the board and employees) that action is being taken to remedy the decline in sales.

Attributing a brand's success or failure to its Distinctive Assets creates two problems. The first is that it can blind you to the real cause of the growth or decline, which means you aren't solving the right problem, or learning from success to be able to replicate it. The second is that it leads to unnecessary change—which is likely to damage the brand's long-term identity.

Distinctive Assets don't need to be omnipotent to be important. But to use these assets well, you do need a clear understanding of the roles they play. Chapters 3 to 7 cover the role of Distinctive Assets, and how they contribute to brand growth.

Gluttony

Gluttony is overindulgence, to the point of waste. It manifests in brand identity when someone often channels his or her inner designer to 'improve' a brand's identity. Tweaking this and changing that creates a slow death by a thousand cuts, with each change nibbling away at the strength of Distinctive Assets, making it harder for category buyers to identify the brand.

It takes discipline to remain steadfast and resist the urge to feast on change. Chapter 2 covers the underpinnings of how our memory works to create, keep and access memories, and explains why consistency is essential for a strong identity, while Chapter 18 helps you handle pressure to update a brand's Distinctive Assets.

Greed

Greed manifests when brand managers try to build too many Distinctive Assets simultaneously. Each Distinctive Asset is a substantial, long-term, investment to build and sustain in the face of competitor activity. Getting greedy and trying to focus on too many assets at once leads to fragmentation, such that no assets are given sufficient resources to properly develop. Narrowing the possible assets to a few priorities is one of the most important strategic decisions you will make. Chapters 13 to 17 examine the strengths and weaknesses of different types of assets, such as colours, taglines and celebrities, to help in this process.

Sloth

Sloth manifests in the neglect of Distinctive Assets. The natural state of memory is decay, which means Distinctive Assets need to be put to work (be retrieved from people's memories) to remain fresh. Idle Distinctive Assets decline in strength, and this reduces the value of past asset-building investments. Chapter 2 covers how to stave off memory decay while Chapters 8 to 11 provide guidelines and metrics for assessing the strength of Distinctive Assets.

Lust

Lust is that constant craving for the next big thing—whether that be the latest celebrity, technology or even the latest season's colour. This constant desire for the brightest and shiniest leads to focusing on the new, but untested assets and ignoring the older, well-established assets. Siphoning off resources to new assets starves existing assets and leaves them vulnerable to decay and competitor attack. It is crucial to first understand and value the brand's current assets, and then only look to something new when that new asset adds something meaningful to the brand's portfolio. Chapter 12 explains how to craft a cohesive set of assets that work together without unnecessary duplication to drain resources. Chapters 18 and 19 cover how to decide when to add a new asset.

Wrath

Wrath manifests when someone gets caught up in the emotion or meaning, and forgets the major purpose of the asset—which is to trigger the brand in people's minds. The criterion of generating emotion or having an additional rich meaning—or both—as the basis for asset selection not only distracts brand managers, it also leads to investing in assets that will be difficult to own, and not selecting assets that might be emotion- or meaning-neutral, but have more promise as branding devices. Chapter 2 introduces the topic of mental competition, which is integral to this issue, and Chapter 6 covers the role of meaning in Distinctive Asset selection. Chapter 16 applies these ideas to the specific context of celebrities as Distinctive Assets.

Envy

Envy is coveting others' possessions. This is revealed in brand identity when a brand manager or designer turns to competitors to inspire a brand's Distinctive Assets. Imitation is the sincerest form of flattery but knowing how to zag when the competitor zigs is instrumental for building a strong Distinctive Asset. Another key skill is to manage the envy of others, such as when a competitor tries to imitate your brand. Chapter 10 examines the perils of lack of Uniqueness, and what the warning bells are when competitors' performance could have a negative effect on asset-building potential.

The path to redemption

While these sins are common, the good news is most sins can be avoided with a good foundation of knowledge about how Distinctive Assets work. The next chapters lay down the path to that redemption. I hope you find the journey valuable.

2

Creating Distinctive Brand Assets

JENNI ROMANIUK

This chapter is like a pilot for a television show. Pilots, by their introductory nature, tend to be a bit dense in detail, but they serve an important purpose of laying the groundwork for the rest of the series. This chapter sets out the foundation of knowledge that is applied throughout the rest of the book. Before we get into the specific topic of Distinctive Assets, let's first talk about the birds and the bees, or where brands come from . . .

Mummy, Daddy, where do brands come from?

Each bit of knowledge you have sits in your memory as a node within a larger network of ideas. When you encounter something for the first time, if you pay sufficient attention, this experience can create a new node to represent this new bit of knowledge. This new node doesn't exist in isolation, it gets attached to your existing memory network. This idea of human memory is referred to as the collective *associative network theories* of memory (for detail, see Anderson & Bower, 1979). This process of building a network also describes how a brand is created in your memory (Keller, 1993).

Think about the first time you heard of the brand 'Uber'. Perhaps, like me, the word 'Uber' was already a fragile thought in your memory, with a few links to other ideas. I remember thinking it meant something extreme, with vague German connotations, but that's it. You then probably learnt Uber is like a taxi, which helped you put the brand 'Uber' in the 'things I pay to take me places' part of your brain, currently occupied by taxis, trains and buses, rather than, say, a brand of ice cream or a bank.

Over time your memory evolved other associations, as you encountered the brand, the mobile app, the drivers, the pricing system and so on. These associations also come from advertising, stories in the media, and conversations with others. Perhaps you signed on and used Uber, which led you to develop specific associations for your individual experiences with booking rides and drivers. As you engaged with Uber, specific trips converted into general brand associations, such as 'friendly drivers', rather than remembering each individual driver, or 'quick response', rather than remembering each waiting time (for more on this process, see Winocur, Moscovitch & Bontempi, 2010).

MY FIRST UBER EXPERIENCE

I remember my first Uber experience. I took a car with a friend from Brooklyn to Manhattan on a Sunday night, with Darryl (our driver) and his black SUV. We had an entertaining conversation with him about his three lady friends that he regularly picked up. He also helped us find a bar open in midtown late on a Sunday night.

What was your first Uber experience? Or if you have not used Uber, think about some other category where you learnt about a brand for the first time. What can you remember? Now contrast the detail of that experience with, say, one that is more routine. Chances are the detail is much less rich, as your brain has consolidated that specific experience into your general memory network.

Other brand associations also form. These associations include Distinctive Assets, which are associations that help you to identify the brand with ease: colours (black), font (FF Clan) and images such as the app thumbnail. The broader memory network for the brand takes form and this network becomes a reservoir of knowledge that you can potentially utilise each time you encounter either the brand (seeing an advertisement) or a situation where the brand is something that could be useful to you (needing to travel to the airport).

Forming memories about Distinctive Assets

Our memory is where we store past experiences for future use.

We don't *need* to use our memory to store past experiences: we could do a *Memento*[1], and write notes and place them in strategic places, and tattoo important information on our body. We could also ask others to remind us, but these systems are very inefficient compared to the portability and power of our own brain. But the efficiency of our brain comes at a price— a price paid in errors in noticing and remembering. These errors, which are detrimental to the creation of memories, are the cost of doing business with the brain (Tulving & Craik, 2000).

We can store memories for utilitarian reasons, such as to remember the restaurant with excellent Thai food. We can also store for emotional reasons, such as to remember how a first kiss felt. Sometimes we deliberately store information, such as when rehearsing a password, while on other occasions memory storage is inadvertent, such as when something takes us by surprise. Factors such as rehearsing pertinent information improve our memory's performance but our memories are always fallible, and become even more likely to be forgotten as time elapses from the event (Craik & Watkins, 1973).

Why might someone store a Distinctive Asset in his or her memory? For example how is it beneficial for me to know Starbucks is also a circular image of a white lady on a green background? This is an easy question to answer as I walked down the street this morning looking for a nice place to sit and have a coffee. While I am sure there were many options I went past, all I saw in my pre-caffeine haze was the Starbucks logo, like a beacon on the street. I didn't need to think, which is good, because it is rare that my pre-caffeine thoughts are of any value; I just found something that worked at that time.

---

1   The 2000 movie staring Guy Pearce, directed by Christopher Nolan.

My own coffee-fuelled experiences aside, for consumers, generally the key benefit of remembering Distinctive Assets is often utilitarian: to help that person find the brand with ease when a future need, where that brand could be the answer, arises. This makes Distinctive Assets that help get the brand found in its shopping environment particularly valuable for both the buyer and, as a consequence, the brand.

Shopping environments include in-store, online, on a street, in a mall, on a mobile phone, and Distinctive Assets can play an important role as a mental short cut for identification in all these arenas. While shoppers have a small incentive to learn about a brand's Distinctive Assets to quicken shopping time, this is not a strong motivating force. The majority of shoppers have a repertoire of brands that they buy, and one brand not found can be easily substituted by another. Therefore *there is little penalty for the buyer* if a specific brand is difficult to find, as a suitable alternative is often available (Sharp, 2010a). *The brand pays a much higher price if it is not easily found*, as it loses sales to a competitor (more on assets in shopping environments in Chapter 5).

Other non-shopping environments are those the brand appropriates to build up and freshen consumers' mental structures (Ehrenberg et al., 2002). These include media platforms such as television, YouTube or radio, social media platforms such as Facebook, Instagram or Snapchat, or events such as the Olympics, or food or music festivals. Distinctive Assets in these environments expand beyond shopping assets to also include creative-based assets, such as jingles or characters. In these non-shopping environments, the consumer lacks an explicit motive to work hard to identify the brand. The onus is on the marketer and the agency to work hard to ensure that the brand is a noticeable part of any execution.

This hard work by the marketer is necessary as memory storage is a capricious process. Most aspects of our everyday experiences don't make the cut, and simply pass by our long-term memory. This means it is up to marketers to make sure the brand is something that makes it through the attention filter we use to simplify our lives. For Distinctive Assets to do their branding job, these assets need to be linked to the brand in the memory of category buyers. This means both the Distinctive Asset and the brand need to be noticeable for Distinctive Assets to be first formed, and then reinforced over time to further freshen the link.

This means the brand's Distinctive Assets typically emerge from the effective decisions marketers make about where and how to place the brand name and the asset together. Over time the link between the asset and the brand strengthens such that even without the brand present, the Distinctive Asset triggers the brand in the memory of category buyers. The greater the number of people with this link between the asset and the brand name, the greater the number of category buyers who could trigger the brand. This is why Fame, which is a measure of how many category buyers think of the brand when exposed to the asset, is a key measure of Distinctive Asset strength (more detail on this in Chapter 9).

Anchor new items into memory

The start of the chapter talked about the process for new items entering memory, and how the familiar aspects of an experience anchor the new parts of the experience into specific locations within the memory network. The substance of this anchor is crucial as it influences both the meaning of the new information, and when and how the new item will be remembered. This same process happens for the formation of Distinctive Assets, and this highlights the importance of the brand as the anchor for where the Distinctive Asset sits in memory. Distinctive Assets *can* be anything sensory—sight, sound, smell, touch—as long as the first important step occurs, which is to anchor the asset with a brand name that is already present in memory[2]. This anchoring gives the asset the meaning of the brand, which is necessary for the Distinctive Asset's future ability to substitute for the brand name, and this also gives the brand some protection from competitors copying an asset. While we can use assets

---

2   For Distinctive Assets to form, the brand name needs to be already in memory. If your brand does not have widespread recognition, then it is advisable to work on building brand awareness before building Distinctive Assets, as the level of prompted awareness will form a ceiling on how strong a brand's assets can become.

independently of the brand, not having a brand name link means that if a competitor launches a similar version, the brand is vulnerable as people don't realise they didn't buy the brand they had initially intended to buy. It is therefore much harder to argue that consumers were misled by the new entrant's design.

Every day people around the world are forming new memories, even for established brands. No one is born with knowledge of Distinctive Assets. Marketers have to work to create the conditions whereby these assets are learnt, and the brand as an anchor is crucial to this.

Memories are defined by the company they keep

Once links with a brand name are formed, Distinctive Assets sit in the brand's network of associations along with other linked attributes (as described in Keller, 1993). For example when I think of 'Apple' a flood of thoughts enters my brain. These range from the products (MacBook Pro, iPhone, Apple Watch), people (Steve Jobs, Michael Fassbender, even my colleague Byron Sharp), services (Genius Bar that I have visited several times with computer emergencies, the iTunes store), to the Distinctive Assets of the logo and white headphones. Oh and yes, I still think of Apple as a fruit, and 'pie' is in there too, which takes me to a different part of my brain, focused on dessert!

Our memory network helps us to remember, imagine, infer and solve problems, from how to fix a broken window to ways to rehydrate after exercise. We mentally delve into our past until we reach something useful to apply in our present moment. If nothing useful emerges, we might seek out help from another source (hello Google!) or just move onto another thought, if the idea or problem was of lesser importance.

We rarely remember for the sake of remembering; we usually remember for a specific purpose. And for most categories that purpose is to buy something to satisfy an open objective, such as hunger, thirst, self-expression or something more prosaic, such as to clean the floor. This idea of memory with a purpose is important, as it highlights that each time, some remembering will be more useful than others. Not all associations are equally useful in all situations.

A (known) brand is a node in memory, with other linked attributes and associations. These attributes and associations don't sit in isolation but are also linked to other parts of memory. For example when I think of Apple Watch, I think of my friend Magda who has one, and then I think of her father who bought her the gift, which then leads me to think of the lovely Easter I spent at their house in Poland and so on. Distinctive Assets are a subcategory of these linked ideas—the identification tools that can trigger the brand name, in its absence.

Figure 2.1: Example of my associative network of memories for Apple, including Distinctive Assets

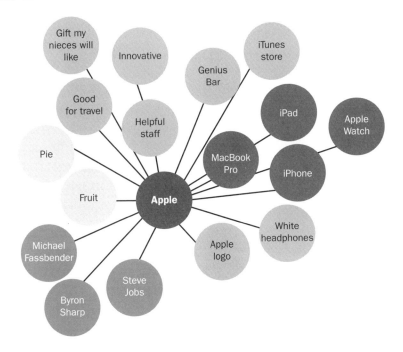

You remember with your memories

To access our memories we need a point of entry, or cue. Thoughts attached to the cue used to enter the memory network compete with each other for retrieval, and therefore the cue shapes what is first *available* to be retrieved (Collins & Loftus, 1975; Holden, 1993). For example when you think of the word *chocolate*, is your mind flooded with thoughts? What about the word *hungry*? Again you probably had a flood of thoughts as your memory danced down connected neurons. Finally how about the cue, *something to give the kids to eat*? What comes to mind with this thought?

Each of these thoughts acts as a cue into your memory network. While each cue differs, their networks overlap when common, salient, connections are present: for example perhaps you thought of Snickers for both cues of *chocolate* and *hungry*?

Just as noticing or encoding information into memory has its quirks, retrieval is better thought of in terms of chances rather than certainties. Nothing is ever guaranteed to be remembered: think of how many times you have forgotten a name, a birthday or an anniversary. The factors that drive this chance of retrieval are freshness and consistency.

Freshness, relative to (mental) competition

We don't remember everything stored in our memory at any single point in time. As our memory is a big interconnected network, without a natural stopping mechanism we would become buried in our, increasingly irrelevant, thoughts. Our brain limits the energy devoted to accessing memories in any specific circumstance, so we don't exhaust our mental resources deciding on lunch (Collins & Loftus, 1975). Only a few items make the mental leap from long-term memory into working memory (Anderson, 1983).

To have the best chance of being retrieved, your brand needs to be more accessible (fresher[3]) than competitive options. Otherwise buyers could run out of energy before they get to your brand. Distinctive Assets give the brand more pathways to retrieval, but, while a brand could gather a large number of Distinctive Assets, the need to keep assets fresh or accessible puts a limit on the sustainable number of assets.

Freshness matters, but so also does the number of other memories also fighting for retrieval. The greater the number of other (non–brand name) memories linked to the Distinctive Asset, the lower the chance the brand will be retrieved (known as the 'fan effect': Anderson & Reder, 1999).

---

3   The analogy of freshness is useful because it reminds us that it is natural for memories to decay over time, and so go stale, like bread.

Competitor memories are not just competitors' brand names, but any other ideas the asset triggers. For example I see the picture of a dachshund on a bag from the sleepware retailer Peter Alexander and I think of my own dachshund puppy, Alfie, who looks very similar, and this creates a flood of non–Peter Alexander–related memories. The brand not only has to fight to keep fresher than *competitors' brands*, but also fresher than *any memories* linked to its Distinctive Assets. This is a key reason why it is riskier for a brand to try to cultivate Distinctive Assets with rich meaning (Chapters 6 and 16 explore this in more detail in the context of assets used for positioning, and for celebrities as Distinctive Assets).

The importance of understanding the level and nature of mental competition is apparent in the frequency with which this idea appears throughout the book. A measure of the level of mental competition that exists is Uniqueness, which is also a key metric for assessing Distinctive Asset strength.

Consistency

Consistency, which is the act of doing the same thing over time, gets mixed reviews in branding strategy. At times, consistency is celebrated as one of the brand's strengths, while at other times dismissed as a weakness, symptomatic of a lack of innovation. One of the most important findings in recent times about our long-term memories is that they change over time. Previous thinking was that once something was in our long-term memory, it was fixed, immutable and always retrieved and put back in pristine condition (Sacktor, 2014). Recent research has shown that long-term memories are vulnerable to contamination from the conditions when they are retrieved (Kitamura et al., 2017).

For example if I remember a memory with a sad emotion attached when I am in a happy mood, the happy emotional conditions of retrieval contaminate the past memory, and return that memory back to long-term storage a little less sad. Similarly, if I see my sister in a red top and am reminded of an event where she was wearing a blue top, the current experience of her in the red top can overwrite the past visual of her in the blue top. Therefore, the next time I access that memory, my sister wears a red top, not a blue one. Many of your childhood memories are very different from the actual experience you had. As a test for this, compare your memory of a childhood event with that of someone else there at the same time. You will find you both remember the same event differently. Part of this is what you noticed at the time, but part of it is also that each of you has different retrieval experiences that have changed these memories.

This means our memories are not fixed but evolve over time. If the new exposure is consistent with the past, each new act of retrieval can strengthen prior memories. But inconsistencies can influence past memories, and change or weaken the links to a brand. This happens to memories of Distinctive Assets too, which are vulnerable to pressure to change and update (Newstead, 2014). While often the benefits of these changes are detailed, it is rare for marketers to consider the cost of inconsistency, and this cost is paid in the future (reduced) strength of the branding in buyer memory.

Keeping a Distinctive Asset consistent means each new exposure builds on the past and the Distinctive Asset links strengthen in memory, making it easier for the category buyer to identify the brand in any situation. In contrast, inconsistencies between the past and the present create multiple traces that become side paths that can lead category buyers astray mentally (Hintzman, 1988; Hintzman & Block, 1971; McClelland & Chappell, 1998). Throughout *Building Distinctive Brand Assets*, instances where consistency is paramount are highlighted, as well as when there might be some freedom to vary assets.

The next chapter discusses the general roles of branding and Distinctive Assets, which are then explored in more detail over Chapters 4 to 7.

3

Why Distinctive Assets Matter

JENNI ROMANIUK

Strong Distinctive Assets require a long-term commitment to create and maintain the necessary memories. This chapter covers why branding is important and why building Distinctive Assets is a useful investment in time and effort.

How and why we brand

Branding, or the act of attaching a name to something, has occurred since the first craftsperson signalled 'I made this' by etching a name into their handiwork. Branding today goes not only on the product but also on peripheral material, such as advertising, social media and promotional activities. Each different branding environment creates executional challenges that the brand needs to overcome to be noticed.

Three primary reasons for engaging in the act of branding are to stamp the brand's *ownership*, *anchor* desired associations to the brand's part of the memory network for category buyers, and act as a *bridge* between disparate marketing activities. These three roles apply to both the brand name, and the brand's Distinctive Assets.

Figure 3.1: The three roles of branding

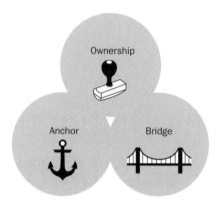

Branding role 1: Proclaiming ownership

The presence of a brand proclaims that item's ownership. It's the marketing equivalent of signing your painting; it tells the world 'our company produced this'. Branding goes beyond the actual product, and there are many examples of branded items:

- an image or link on an online store
- a shop on the street
- a job advertisement
- a hashtag
- a carry bag
- an annual report
- company merchandise (T-shirts, hats, pens).

These items can all contain the brand to signal its owner. With the arrival of new media, new branding opportunities present themselves: for example some restaurants are putting their brand on meals so that the restaurant name is identifiable when customers post pictures on Instagram (Krader, 2017).

The presence of a known brand also marks something as familiar. Because of our tendency to pay attention to the familiar (Harrison, 2013), the branded item is a bit more likely to catch our eye or ear than other unfamiliar stimuli also competing for attention in that same environment. Janiszewski, Kuo and Tavassoli (2013) have a useful analogy of a series of paintbrushes trying to paint a scene: the viewers' attention directs the brain to fill in the picture for familiar items first, and away from unfamiliar items. This leads to quicker recognition of the familiar, which refreshes the memory of the brand or can lead to purchase.

Ownership is also a necessary condition for the other two benefits of branding: as an anchor or bridge.

Branding role 2: Anchoring knowledge in memory

The brand can act as an anchor for messages in memory. The presence of the brand is how new brand messages get put into the brand part of memory, to be remembered by the category buyer in buying situations (Anderson, 1983). The process for this depends on the combination of familiar or new concepts embedded within an experience.

First, let's take the example of linking together two familiar concepts. If you see a sign saying McDonald's is now serving tacos—and you are familiar with McDonald's, and also familiar with the concept of a taco—the exposure creates a link between the two. Now if you think of tacos, a (new) possibility—McDonald's—will come to mind, and vice versa. Without the presence of the brand *McDonald's*, the experience will be anchored in the taco part of your brain only, which is of little benefit to McDonald's next time you feel like a taco.

Even prior messages still need to be anchored to the brand; this is so a brand can have a fresher link than competitive options, and overcome mental competition. For example if I see an advertisement for breakfast, I might remember that great breakfast I had last week with a friend whom I hadn't seen for a long time. But if I see an advertisement for breakfast *at McDonald's*, this freshens the link between breakfast and McDonald's in my memory. Both the specific episode with a friend and McDonald's are linked to *breakfast* in my brain, but *McDonald's* only gets freshened when I notice the presence of *McDonald's*.

When the stimuli combination changes from all familiar to something familiar and something new, the familiar part of the stimuli anchors the experience, and the novel component will become attached at this node in memory. For example you see a computer bag with the name *Florgen* embossed on its handle. You are familiar with the concept of a computer bag but have never heard of the brand *Florgen*. *Florgen* therefore enters your memory in the 'computer bag' part of your brain, and this provides the context for this new brand. So when you encounter the *Florgen* brand again, this can cue *computer bag* and vice versa.

We have problems in retaining information when both concepts are new. The lack of an anchor means the experience is difficult to remember. For example if you listen to two people speaking Flemish, and you don't understand Flemish, you don't remember the conversation because the words said have no context to attach to in your existing memory network. Likewise, when a new brand is launched, the unknown brand has no context in memory until the mental structures that ground the brand in the category are developed. Only after that can the new brand move onto building Distinctive Assets. For example if I don't know what Airbnb offers, the value in me seeing the logo for Airbnb over and over again is small. This is also why if a brand has low prompted brand awareness with the category cue, it is crucial to improve that metric *before* building Distinctive Assets.

An anchor helps things settle in the right place.

When the brand acts as an anchor, attached information gets put in the 'brand' part of someone's memory. What happens when the brand fails to gain attention? If the brand is not the anchor, something else may take its place:

- the product category ('an advertisement for smartphones')
- a creative element ('the advertisement Johnny Depp is in')
- the location or media where it was encountered ('the advertisement I saw on the way to work')
- some other situational factor ('at the cinema seeing that Star Wars movie').

While these descriptions might help record the advertising exposure in category buyers' memories, the lack of linkage to the brand means memory of this advertising doesn't refresh or cue the brand[1]. This reduces the value of advertising exposure, often to nothing. To have an immediate or subsequent impact, marketing activities need to be designed with the brand to act as an anchor.

Branding role 3: Bridging activities with a common origin

The presence of the brand signals that different activities have a common origin. In this way, the brand acts as a bridge for otherwise seemly disparate items. This disparity can be in place, time, content or message. For example:

- *multi-platform campaigns*—the brand can bridge across different activities across media, such as a television advertisement and a Facebook advertisement.
- *messaging*—the brand can bridge across executions with different messages, such as a bank's advertisement for a new home loan rate, and another execution about a deal for a credit card.
- *campaigns*—the brand can bridge across new creative with past creative, such as Geico Insurance's advertising with the cavemen and its advertising with the gecko.
- *multi-channel distribution*—the brand can bridge across distribution channels such as in-store and online, such as Cadbury Chocolate's placement in Tesco supermarkets and its presence in Tesco's online store.

Branding can also connect across these four areas: for example by connecting a message on social media with an in-store activity, or the presence of the brand in an e-commerce store with the campaign seen last year. Figure 3.2 illustrates the bridging roles available to the brand. This capacity to act as a bridge requires consistent branding, so that the bridge is easily apparent, sturdy. If the bridge is flimsy, someone is more likely to fall off the retrieval path than reach the other side.

---

1   This is also why we need to be careful about advertising effectiveness metrics that rely on memory for the advertisement rather than memory for the branded advertisement. Just because an exposure entered memory doesn't mean it entered in a useful part of memory.

Figure 3.2: The bridging roles of the brand

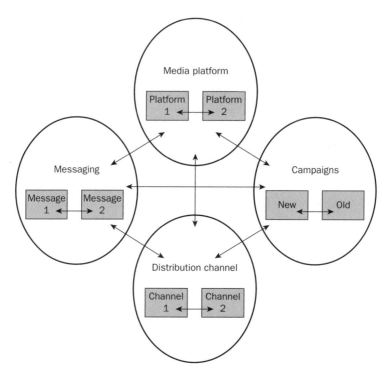

The (added) value of Distinctive Assets

The power of a Distinctive Asset is that it can act as a proxy for the brand, and so, if sufficiently strong, can achieve the same ownership, anchor and bridge roles. In addition to these three roles, Distinctive Assets provide a brand with a wider range of options to determine *how* someone experiences the brand. The nature of Distinctive Assets provides three additional benefits to help the brand break through and get noticed: *flexibility*, *adaptability* and *neurological diversity*.

Figure 3.3: The added value of Distinctive Assets

Within-execution flexibility

With every piece of brand collateral, someone decides *how* to brand. Size, placement, mode, timing and level of integration are all conscious decisions. But it is rare that branding decisions are made in isolation; branding is often sold short by a *perceived* trade-off between strong branding and excellent creative—that to get one, the brand needs to sacrifice the other (this trade-off is an illusion, as discussed in Chapter 4).

Distinctive Assets provide an alternative way, one that might help get the best of both worlds. By representing the brand in non–brand name forms, Distinctive Assets can be perceived as less intrusive and allow effective branding execution, without anyone feeling the need to sacrifice creative quality.

Distinctive Assets can work with the creative aspects of the advertisement to maximise the brand's anchoring potential at key moments. For example in a television advertisement, an audio Distinctive Asset, such as Dennis Haysbert's voice for Allstate Insurance, can signal the brand while the visual image communicates the message. This helps the message represented by the image get anchored into the part of memory where the brand sits.

Other multi-modal examples include having music signalling the brand in the background while demonstrating a new usage situation or a spokesperson representing the brand in visual form while verbalising the message. This flexibility of brand execution opens up a wider range of branding moment opportunities, thereby increasing the footprint of the brand within the advertisement and making it easier for people to correctly identify the advertised brand.

This flexibility extends beyond advertising, to execution of packaging. As pack format changes, so too can the brand's Distinctive Assets. For example the packaging shape for snacking or single-use items often differs from the sharing or multi-use options. In the smaller size, simple visual assets might work better to grab people's attention than word-based items, such as the brand or tagline assets that are more difficult to read if shrunk to fit on a smaller pack.

Adaptability to different platforms

Distinctive Assets allow you to adapt the branding to better stand out in different media and channel environments. What works to make the brand stand out in one platform might not work in another. In advertising, the brand needs to stand out in an environmental spectrum that ranges from visually rich print to audio-only radio; from text-rich newspapers to pictures in magazines; and from where the advertisement dominates the media such as television, to just a small part of a cluttered content space such as an online banner advertisement; and across devices ranging from large-screen televisions to mobile phone screens. In retail channels, the brand representation can vary from tangible physical forms in-store, to small thumbnail images in an online or mobile environment.

With Distinctive Assets you can tailor the branding to work best on a particular platform. In each representation, the brand needs to be able to break through and command viewer attention *at least once*. By providing alternative ways to represent the brand, building Distinctive Assets means the brand can have a better chance of cutting through clutter specific to that platform.

Global brands have a heightened need to adapt to a wide range of different platforms. Distinctive Assets can work across cultures, differing levels of literacy, and for countries with non-roman texts such as Russia, Japan, South Korea or China. And in today's global travel world, Distinctive Assets help a person who does not speak the language find a familiar brand, something I notice McDonald's often implements well with its signage and advertising.

Understanding the audience's experiences on the platform and how these affect what is likely to be noticed is key to a successful adaptation of assets. Copy that looks good on a computer screen or on a printed sheet of paper can fail in real life. For example at an awards function I attended, the winners stood in front of the company banner for a picture. The banner had been designed with the brand name and logo in the centre. This meant that for the photographs, the people standing in front of the banner covered up the brand and none of the postings on various media outlets featured the brand. This was a lost opportunity, as many more people would see the photographs than actually attended the event. Simply putting the brand name on the top of the banner, so it could also be seen in the context of photograph taking, would have overcome this issue.

Outdoor highway advertising also features common examples of misguided brand execution, where often the prime space is given to the message, rather than the brand. Think about the audience, which is someone driving by on their way from one destination to another, often travelling at a reasonably fast speed. The driver has just a quick glance to process the advertisement before returning attention to the road. If the brand is not part of that quick glance, those few seconds of attention are wasted.

To understand the influence of the context, here are some questions to consider:

- How far away will people be from the brand? How will this vary?
- What clutter will compete with the brand for attention, and how can this be overcome?

  —Other creative elements?

  —Other brands, other people?

  —Other non-related items in the environment (for example cars)?

- Is this clutter static or moving? How does the branding visibility change with this?
- Are there any other conditions that change the nature of clutter, such as time of day, weather, co-consumption activities?

It is not just advertising platforms: today's multi-channel distribution world means a brand needs to stand out in different competitive retail environments. First, think of a hypermarket, where the brand might sit on big shelves next to competitor brands, and compare that to a corner store, where the brand might sit alone or next to other similar product categories, in the household or food section. Then also consider online retailers and the non-brand clutter that surrounds the brand on the two-dimensional screen. For those of you who work in service categories, look at the environment on the brand's own website versus the street (if the brand has retail branches) versus the environment a broker experiences.

Once you understand how the brand sits in each of these different contexts, you can draw on the brand's Distinctive Assets to adapt executions so the brand can stand out to as many people as possible in each context.

Neurological diversity

The brand name, as a word, has a narrow neurological impact but the brand name as Distinctive Asset can open up a (brand) new world. Experiencing stimuli is a multifaceted neurological event similar to watching an orchestra play music. Our eyes take in the visual components, our ears the audio components and, depending on the circumstances, other senses such as smell or touch can also be activated. And within each sense, different parts of the brain can be activated. For example the fusiform face area of the brain lights up when we see a face (Kanwisher, McDermott & Chun, 1997), while other specific parts of the brain are used when we process colour, motion, spatial position and, curiously, when we recognise human body parts (Bernard & Gage, 2007).

To visualise neurological diversity, imagine sitting in a coffee shop and the different stimuli, such as colours, sounds and images, are all individual arrows directed at your brain. Many of these arrows are disregarded by your brain's filtering system (for example the sound of the air conditioning, murmurings from people nearby); others are flagged as worthy of attention and raised to the level of consciousness, but then deemed as non-actionable (someone laughing at the next table). Some are contemplated and thought about a bit more: such as a familiar song playing in the background or, if you see someone who looks like a childhood friend, your brain might activate a childhood memory. Other arrows slip through conscious filters but are processed at a subconscious level in an automatic manner, such as a count of how many people are in the room (as in Hasher & Zacks, 1984).

Every environment is an assault on the senses. Our brain learns to deal with this by being quick, but willing to sacrifice the detail. This means we can miss something next to us, if the brain disregards it as unimportant. It is hard to tell what will grab us at any point in time; sometimes it can be the most trivial thing, like a loose thread on a shirt, or it can be something important, like your child wandering onto the road. Our brain helpfully prioritises some arrows and ignores the rest so we don't use up all of our conscious energy on too many inconsequential things. This filtering process also happens with the environments where we experience a brand.

When a brand is present, it could be one arrow or as multiple arrows, depending on the diversity of representation. For example Geico, as just the brand name, is one arrow, but Geico's Distinctive Asset character, which is a gecko, coloured bright green, with a face, and a distinctive voice, might be four arrows (animal, colour, face and audio) instead of just one. Each of these four arrows can hit different parts of the brain, giving the brand a greater chance of penetrating memory in the face of other competition in the environment: if the brand has both a visual and an audio arrow, then the audio arrow still might get through, even if someone's eyes are distracted. If you have a brand that is represented by a face and a word both next to a puppy, then the face arrow might break through over the competition for attention from the puppy, even if the word arrow does not. Distractions are always going to vary across people and time. A neurologically diverse set of Distinctive Assets gives the brand more opportunity to present itself in such as way that more of the audience will be receptive, and stimulate more brand activity in their brains.

The next chapter examine how Distinctive Assets help build *mental availability*, which is the propensity for the brand to be thought of in buying situations (Romaniuk, 2016a).

4

How Distinctive Assets Build Mental Availability

JENNI ROMANIUK

You first need to be in a race to have any chance of winning it.

Mental availability (also referred to as *brand salience*) is a brand's propensity to be thought of or come to mind in buying situations (Romaniuk, 2016a; Romaniuk & Sharp, 2004). When a brand becomes mentally available in a buying situation, it takes that first crucial step toward being bought.

Think of mental availability as the brand-strategy equivalent of an athlete qualifying for the Olympics. An athlete needs to first qualify for the Olympics to have any chance at winning a gold medal. Someone could run 100 metres faster than Usain Bolt ever did, but without that first qualifying step—no Olympic gold medal. Of course qualifying doesn't guarantee someone a gold medal, as the performance on the day matters; the only certainty is that *not* qualifying means *not winning* a gold medal. Performance on the day is discussed in more detail during the next chapter, which looks at Distinctive Assets' contribution when building *physical availability*.

When incorporated into the branding strategy of any consumer touch-point, Distinctive Assets can increase the presence of the brand.

Touch-points can range from advertising to social media to point of sale in-store. This means that the Distinctive Assets that build mental availability vary widely, and can include colours, words, images, people or audio assets (such as music or jingles), as well as the use in advertising of assets that can also help the brand stand out in shopping environments (such as pack shape).

This chapter explains how Distinctive Assets contribute to building mental availability. While the chapter's focus is on Distinctive Assets, it also includes evidence to challenge some common assumptions about the effect of brand-name execution on advertising effectiveness. Addressing these assumptions is important as they have a detrimental effect on the execution of Distinctive Assets, as well as the brand name.

The brand as an anchor for key advertising messages

An important role of advertising is to build up key mental structures, to increase a brand's chance of being mentally available in buying situations (Ehrenberg et al., 2002). Therefore to build mental availability, also referred to as salience, in buying situations[1], the messages in advertising need to draw from the cues that category buyers use to access, from their memory, possible brands to buy in that situation. By freshening the link to those memories, the brand becomes more mentally available.

These cues are referred to as *category entry points* (CEPs) (Romaniuk, 2016a). They comprise the thoughts that a category buyer has as she stops being just Katie, and transitions into the category-buyer hot zone of Katie the laundry-detergent buyer. For example I drink coffee, so you could consider me a 'coffee category buyer', but I am not in the hot zone of coffee category buying at 11 p.m. (as caffeine keeps me awake). But 11 a.m. is a very different story—every day I transition from being Jenni

---

1   The term *mental availability* is used, rather than *salience*, to avoid the misconception that the discussion is about *top-of-mind awareness* (TOMA). Although we did originally use this term (Romaniuk & Sharp, 2003a; Romaniuk & Sharp, 2004) and tried to point out that the concept of salience is different from the operationalisation of TOMA, there are still many misconceptions about how to measure salience. The use of a new term for the concept is an effort to separate the important step of retrieval from memory in buying situations from the narrow measure of TOMA and the general concept of being prominent in memory (Alba & Chattopadhyay, 1986).

to Jenni the coffee buyer (if I don't have coffee, I transition into Jenni not the best person to have conversation with!).

These 11 a.m.s vary in the mental shift that characterises my entry into the category-buying hot zone—some days I am working from home, so close-by locations where I feel comfortable turning up in my sweatpants get mental priority; other times I am on my way to the office, so I think of places en route where I get something quick; while other times my sleep has been wretched, so I am thinking about where to get a strong coffee. With each of these shifts in context, the set of brands that become mentally available also varies (see also Desai & Hoyer, 2000; Holden, 1993).

CEPs represent the myriad of thoughts that can become cues to access options from memory. A brand attached to these cues has a chance of becoming mentally available, making CEPs valuable mental structures for the brand to build. While CEPs can be associated with the brand, they are not associations *about* the brand. While on the surface this difference might seem semantic, it has a practical importance for both strategy and research.

First, let's cover the strategic implications. The more CEPs the brand is attached to, the greater the number of retrieval pathways available to the brand. For brand strategy this means that setting a goal of accumulating and broadening the brand's CEP network is more effective in building mental availability than a traditional strategy of trying to own a single attribute (or in this case CEP[2]). For example if I am an airline, I want to be known as good for business travellers, good for families, great for getting airline miles, good for budget travellers and so on. Efforts to have airlines that only focus on one CEP, such as for business travel only, continue to fail, even as demand for business travel increases (Calder, 2016). Part of the reason for this is that those who travel for business also take family holidays and, like me, sometimes even go solo backpacking to places such as Africa.

---

2   This is one of the biggest mistakes that marketers make when adopting a CEP strategy, in that they revert back to wanting to own a CEP for the brand. This means they get the right brand message but the wrong brand strategy. It is particularly prevalent in companies with a portfolio of brands, who want to allocate a specific CEP to each brand; this is again misguided and a simple analysis of how brands compete on each CEP reveals why this is an unfeasible strategy. Most of this is due to confusion between Distinctive Assets and CEPs.

The evidence for the need for linkages to many CEPs comes from research that compares the CEP networks of big and small brands. This research shows the big difference between larger- and smaller-share brands is in the number of CEPs that category buyers attach to each brand (Romaniuk, 2016a). And when researchers model the relationships of single attributes and compare this with the results of the brand's total network size with brand choice[3], the total network size has a stronger relationship with future buyer behaviour (Romaniuk, 2003; Romaniuk & Sharp, 2003a, b).

Now let's discuss the research implications. The nature of these associations means we need to consult the category buyer's and user's experience to find CEPs, rather than look to thoughts specifically about any brands. For example when we develop questions to elicit CEPs, these questions focus on aspects such as the when, where, with whom, how someone felt before, during or after, and the why of the buyer's or user's experience (as described in Romaniuk, 2016a). We only ask about a specific brand when it is useful to help the category buyer to better access past memories for a specific experience.

Table 4.1 shows some of the CEPs identified from category buyers in the champagne category, from research into samples of category buyers from the USA conducted in July 2016. These CEPs illustrate a wide range of potential options, from celebration to indulgence to just enjoying a sunny afternoon. But not all options have an equal chance of being

Table 4.1: Examples of category entry points for champagne

When	Where	With whom	How feeling	Why
Having a drink before dinner	For a birthday	For a special moment with a partner	To give me a lift if feeling down/ flat	To recognise a success or achievement
Looking for a nightcap	When out dancing	To open when friends come over	Feeling celebratory	As a gift
To accompany good food	At a bar/ nightclub	When I am by myself	When I want to feel luxurious	Enjoying a sunny afternoon

---

3   Most research assumes the primacy of one model; rarely are competing models compared.

encountered; a second stage of research is needed to understand which are more commonly encountered, and therefore offer more sales opportunities for the brand. Each of these CEPs can be incorporated in the brand's various touch-points.

CEPs can be represented in a variety of audio and visual forms, which mean CEPs often offer a rich field of creative ideas to mine. In audio form, people can be talking or singing; in visual form, CEPs can be represented in a scene or as words on screen. For example a CEP for coffee can be 'to get you through something a bit boring', which is when you grab a coffee just to have something to do to keep you distracted in, say, a boring meeting. This CEP could be shown in visual scenes, such as someone in a workplace looking in dread at a meeting full of people and in words at the bottom of the screen (#facetheboringmeeting). Audio representation could be two people who meet in a lunchroom, talk about the upcoming boring meeting, and either take, or are offered, a coffee. Someone could be falling asleep in a meeting and be nudged awake with a coffee. I am sure if you thought for a few moments, you could come up with many other (most likely much better) ways to also communicate this CEP.

But the CEP message is only one part of building mental availability—the brand is also necessary. Whether the brand name or a Distinctive Asset is used, the presence of the brand ensures the CEP or message gets anchored in the right part of memory. The remainder of this chapter is about another important component: the branding.

Engineering the brand to be noticed in advertising

The low and varying levels of attention of a typical viewer mean just having a brand present is often insufficient for it to have an impact. The brand's presence needs to be engineered to maximise the chance the viewer will notice. This involves executing the brand to overcome two key obstacles:

- *external distractions*, such as the environment, second screens and mental rumination: these hamper attention to the execution (for example Paech, Riebe & Sharp, 2003; Rojas-Mèndez, Davies & Madran, 2009).

- *internal distractions*, or other creative elements, such as animals, music or babies that draw attention away from the brand within the execution (for example Erfgen, Zenker & Sattler, 2015; Pieters & Wedel, 2004).

At each encounter, each viewer needs to only notice the brand once to put it in his or her memory. If everyone behaved similarly, we could therefore execute the brand in one way to overcome that single challenge. But people vary in how they view advertising (Jayasinghe & Ritson, 2013; Paech et al., 2003). Brand execution needs to be sufficiently flexible to overcome the distractions emerging from different types of viewing (and co-viewing) behaviours.

Before talking about Distinctive Assets, I'd like to tackle two myths that hold advertisers back from achieving effective branding, as these misconceptions can also affect how Distinctive Assets are executed.

Myth 1—too much branding ruins an advertisement

A common myth is of a necessary trade-off between branding and creative quality—one will be at the expense of the other. But I have yet to find empirical evidence of a negative relationship between how much branding is in an advertisement, or that how a brand is executed negatively affects viewers; assessment of advertising creative quality. Table 4.2 contains an example from 107 thirty-second television advertisements in Australia.

Table 4.2: Average advertising likeability ratings (1–5 scale) for brand execution tactics for 30-second television advertisements

Visual frequency		Verbal frequency		Entry timing		Duration	
Frequency (times)	Liking	Frequency (times)	Liking	Seconds til brand presence (seconds)	Liking	Time brand is present (seconds)	Liking
1	3.5	1	3.5	<3	3.4	<6	3.5
2	3.3	2	3.5	3–10	3.4	6–8	3.4
3	3.4	3+	3.4	11–21	3.5	9–10	3.4
4	3.7			22+	3.5	11+	3.5
5+	3.5						

Advertising liking, measured as the standard five-point likeability scale (found to drive creative success, as per Haley & Baldinger, 2000), varies little across all different types of brand execution.

Nor is there a relationship between the level of correct branding, which indicates many people noticed the brand being advertised, and viewer assessment of advertising creative quality. Figure 4.1 shows scatter-plot examples of four brands across several years of campaigns (2012–2015), where the percentage of viewers who could correctly identify the brand is plotted against the percentage giving the advertisement a score in the top two boxes of liking (liked or liked a lot). As you can see from the data, the correlations between the two variables are low. Higher correct branding does not lead to lower advertising liking.

Figure 4.1: Examples of the relationship between correct branding scores and advertising liking scores for four different brands (data for executions 2012–2015)

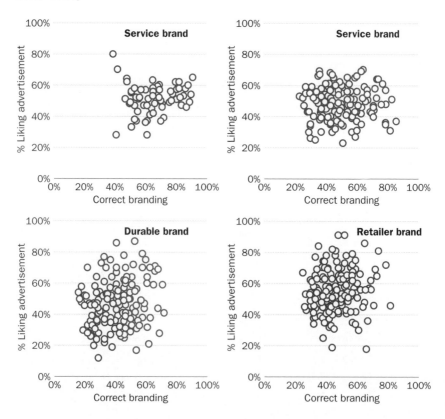

Even viral videos lack any evidence of any negative relationship between branding and the capacity for a viral video to generate high-arousal positive emotions. The presence of the brand is not a barrier to generating the strong, positive emotions that correlate with high sharing of a viral video. For example we found viral videos that generated high-arousal positive emotions showed the brand on average 7.0 times over the duration of the video, while videos with low-arousal positive emotions showed the brand 4.0 times (for more data on this, see Nelson-Field & Romaniuk, 2013, Table 5.4, p. 54).

Of course agencies can create—and marketers can approve—boring advertising, but this is not the fault of the branding.

Myth 2—people will avoid or switch off if the brand is revealed too early

A consistent finding from research into effective branding execution is that early branding leads to higher correct branding (for example see Ogilvy & Raphaelson, 1982; Stewart & Furse, 1986; Stewart & Koslow, 1989; Walker & von Gonten, 1989). Despite this, many advertisements fail to signal the brand early on (as illustrated in Romaniuk, 2009). This mismatch between evidence and action is due to another common myth—that branding early means people will switch off or avoid the advertisement.

Again there is a lack of evidence to support this contention, and quite a bit of evidence to refute it. In the book *Viral Marketing: The Science of Sharing* (Nelson-Field, 2013) we examined whether viral advertising is shared by fewer consumers if it contains more branding. The results show the brand execution tactics observed in the most shared viral videos are indistinguishable from the tactics within the least shared videos. For example the least shared viral videos allowed 34% of the video elapse before showing the brand, while the most shared viral videos allowed 39% of the video elapse before showing the brand (Nelson-Field, 2013, Table 5.3, p. 53). The level of branding, therefore, does *not* affect the sharing of a viral video.

Recently, my colleague Magda Nenycz-Thiel and I examined pre-roll advertising on YouTube, to see if branding in the first five seconds affected ad-skipping rates from the sixth second onwards, which is when viewers can skip the advertising and go straight to the content, and where most of the audience loss takes place. Our testing covered four branding conditions: the brand name only; a Distinctive Asset only; both the brand name and a Distinctive Asset; and no branding at all.

Across 113 video advertisements, the presence of the brand, whether it is the brand name or a Distinctive Asset, had no impact on subsequent audience skipping behaviour (Romaniuk & Nenycz-Thiel, 2017). Figure 4.2 shows that the percentage is around 30% across all forms of brand (or no brand) execution. This again reveals the absence of any evidence that ties the presence of the brand to negative reactions from viewers. Viewers did not excessively flee advertisements with early branding, nor did they reward those without branding.

Figure 4.2: YouTube advertising: early branding and audience-skipping behaviour

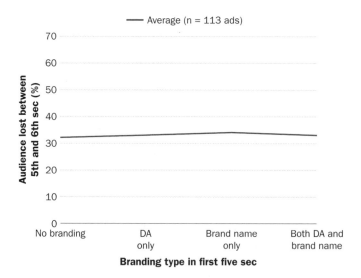

Don't fear the brand: it won't ruin the advertising

Prominent brand inclusion is essential if you want the message to be anchored in the right part of someone's brain. The conclusion from the empirical evidence to date points to it being unnecessary to fear including the brand, whether it be represented as the brand name or a Distinctive Asset. The presence of the brand will not damage the creative quality in the eyes of the audience.

The inclusion of the brand name might still meet resistance—not all people are swayed from their strongly held beliefs by evidence—so one use of Distinctive Assets is to overcome the reluctance of any advertising creative personnel to implement some of the more prominent and effective brand execution techniques. For example using a Distinctive Asset instead of the brand name might overcome concern about putting the brand name at the start of a television advertisement or a viral video. But apart from appeasing the concerns of creative staff, is there evidence of other advantages in using Distinctive Assets instead of the brand name to build mental availability? This is the topic of the next section.

Do Distinctive Assets attract attention to the advertisement or the brand?

A major challenge for any advertisement is to cut through and be noticed by category buyers in today's cluttered, distracting world. One of the reasons given for reticence about using a brand name, particularly early in an advertisement, is that the presence of the brand will put off non-users. This is often based on the presumption that non-users have a negative attitude to the brand and have a reason not to buy. This presumption is contradicted by the considerable evidence that shows it is rare for non-users to hold negative associations for brands and these are usually formed after experience with the brand, so are most commonly held by past users rather than those with no brand experience (Winchester & Romaniuk, 2008; Winchester, Romaniuk & Bogomolova, 2008). Non-users' key characteristic is their lack of thoughts about that non-used brand (Nenycz-Thiel & Romaniuk, 2011; Romaniuk, 2016a).

But perhaps this lack of knowledge is because non-users just switch off when they see the brand's advertising and so don't process anything about the brand. Therefore holding back the brand and drawing non-users in with excellent creative content, before the great brand reveal, will 'trick' non-users into processing the brand's marketing activities. While this hypothesis had been put to me a few times (in particular from advertising executives), I had not seen any evidence, or even testing, of this idea. To see if this idea has any credence, I conducted my own exploratory analysis using a subset of advertisements where I could separate results for brand users and non-users, and the sample size of users was sufficient to get robust results. The advertisements came from a range of common categories including packaged goods, services and durables.

The data set consisted of 42 advertisements of thirty seconds in length; 20 advertisements had the brand name presence in the first third of the advertisement, and 22 did not. Separate cut-through scores for brand users and non-users were created for each advertisement, and the scores for each group averaged. The results (see Figure 4.3) show little difference for either brand users or non-users in cut-through.

Figure 4.3: Early branding and cut-through in television advertising: brand users versus non-users

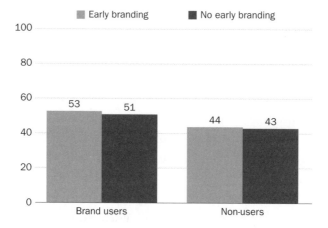

It is always harder for advertising to break through to non-users, when compared to brand users who score higher for advertising recall questions (Harrison, 2013; Vaughan, Beal & Romaniuk, 2016). But holding back the brand is not a remedy for this; it does not increase the advertising's cut-through for non-users.

Unfortunately, due to the nature of this data set, the impact on branding scores and the difference between direct branding and branding via Distinctive Assets could not be tested. But the next study, in online advertising, is able to explore this issue.

This research involved a split sample test of online static advertisements across eight brands with strong Distinctive Assets in the USA. Respondents were split into three groups and shown a series of web pages with news stories in different fonts. The cover story provided was that they were being asked to evaluate the different styles. Embedded in eight different stories were target advertisements for the eight brands[4], and each advertisement had the brand name, a visual Distinctive Asset or a tagline. Respondents only saw one advertisement from each brand but the branding treatment varied across advertisements. At the end of the survey, after a fifteen-minute distractor task, respondents were asked a series of questions about their memories for the target advertising and the brands advertised. At the end of the survey, respondents were also asked about their linkages of the assets used with the target brands, and only those who could link the asset with the brand name were included in the scores for the Distinctive Asset treatment—so the comparison was as much as possible 'apples with apples'.

The results show the advertising with Distinctive Assets had higher cut-through than the advertising with the brand name, with advertising recall at 33% for executions with tagline Distinctive Assets, at 30% for executions with visual Distinctive Assets, and at 27% for executions with the brand name (see Figure 4.4 for example results for three brands, Geico, KFC and Red Bull, and the average results overall). This pattern was consistent for both brand users and non-users.

Figure 4.4: Online banner brand execution and advertisement recall

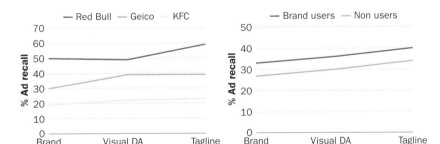

---

4   The experiment involved a split sample test across 1200 US adults in 2017. The stimuli included other advertising that was consistent across treatments, but varied across web pages.

But this advantage for Distinctive Assets is not maintained when asking about the memory for the brand (see Figure 4.5 which shows examples for three brands—McDonald's, Oreos and Nike—as well as the average results across all executions). The results show quite lower brand recognition, measured as the proportion of those who recall seeing the advertisement unbranded who could identify the brand being advertised. The overall brand recognition scores are 32% for executions with the brand name, 23% for executions with visual Distinctive Assets and 17% for executions with taglines. Therefore, while better at grabbing attention, taglines had, on average, around half the brand attribution of the brand name.

Figure 4.5: Online banner brand execution and brand recognition

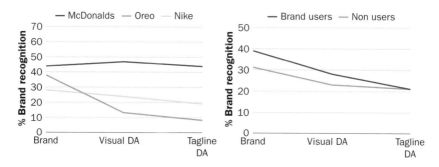

This suggests that while a Distinctive Asset can grab attention in a cluttered online environment such as a news site, this attention advantage is often counteracted by a branding disadvantage. Exceptions can happen, as we found KFC and McDonald's had visual assets that are equal or greater in correct branding than the brand name. But this is not, as yet, the typical result[5].

Now we can turn to print advertising, which, while not as sexy as online media, is still an important component of the media mix. In a full-page print advertising experiment across four categories, research led by my colleague Nicole Hartnett (Hartnett, 2011; Hartnett, Romaniuk

---

5   We are continuing our R&D to work out the conditions when Distinctive Assets succeed more than the brand name. At this stage I would speculate a creative counter-programming element that needs to be considered: that the Distinctive Asset needs to contrast with the style of advertising, so that the Distinctive Asset stands out rather than blends in, but further research is needed to assess this hypothesis.

& Kennedy, 2016) found no difference in the advertising cut-through, whether branding was the brand name, a visual or a word-based Distinctive Asset (see Table 4.3). Overall the brand name is stronger than tagline assets (53% recall versus 25% for tagline assets).

Similar to the results observed with online advertising, we do see variation in the strength of visual Distinctive Assets across categories. In two cases (banking and pasta sauce), the visual assets score at a level that was similar to or greater than the brand name (as shown in Table 4.3). Therefore sometimes a Distinctive Asset can outperform the brand, but it can also just as easily underperform if not well executed.

Table 4.3: Print advertising brand execution, cut-through and brand recall (%)

Ad cut-through	Overall	Banking	Chocolate	Haircare	Pasta sauce
Brand name	64	48	82	61	64
Visual DA	63	53	76	60	62
Tagline DA	60	48	80	57	55
Brand recall	Overall	Banking	Chocolate	Haircare	Pasta sauce
Brand name	53	70	51	36	51
Visual DA	48	81	41	6	51
Tagline DA	25	52	14	7	26

From Hartnett (2011)

Effectively executing Distinctive Assets in advertising

One common factor across all theories of how advertising works is that the identification of the brand that is advertising is necessary for the advertisement to have impact on brand sales[6]. The execution guidelines for any single Distinctive Asset are the same as those for the brand name— the asset needs to be sufficiently noticeable that it can cut through in the face of inattentive viewers.

---

6   Again I have had occasional push back on this, from people claiming that poorly branded advertising can work as advertising for the category, and therefore lift sales for the brand that way. But I presume this means lifting sales for competitors as well, which seems an undesirable outcome, particularly for a small brand. It would be a better use of advertising dollars to shift brand sales but not those of competitors.

Distinctive Assets also enable the branding to adapt to the advertising platform, and provide flexibility within the execution of each piece of creative content. The capacity for Distinctive Assets to add adaptability and flexibility depends on the set of assets a brand has, which is why it is useful to build a Distinctive Asset *palette*, made up of asset types diverse in both their impact on the senses and neurological impact (more on this in Chapter 12). Diversity in the set of asset types simply provides more options for everyone to work with.

In two studies into online and print advertising, the test between Distinctive Assets and the brand name was with a like-for-like execution swap with the brand name. As Distinctive Assets are indirect branding, the chance of retrieval failure exists, as the presence of a link in memory does not guarantee retrieval, only of a non-zero chance. A strong Distinctive Asset can't overcome poor execution. For example in her research, Hartnett found that with Garnier Fructis's bright green, despite its being a strong asset, only 6% of those who recognised the treatment advertisement and knew that bright green is linked to Fructis thought of Fructis when they saw the advertisement (Hartnett, 2011). Therefore where the Distinctive Asset simply replaces the brand name, the risk is that someone could fail to notice the asset or fail to remember the link between the asset and the brand. This means that, while the freshness of the asset-to-brand-name link matters, so too does the quality of execution: the asset needs to be noticeable to be effective.

This highlights a danger when using Distinctive Assets, and that is assuming that Distinctive Assets will be so effective at attracting attention that the brand can sacrifice some of the assets' presence in favour of other creative elements. The evidence from the experiments to date is that Distinctive Assets can fail execution-wise and pass by unnoticed. Therefore while a Distinctive Asset might be a powerful weapon to attract attention, having a powerful weapon is of little value without correct use.

Like-for-like brand- or asset-swap treatments do miss a big advantage of Distinctive Assets, which is as a rich foundation for creative ideas. Building creative content around a Distinctive Asset makes the brand the central part of the advertisement, and so provides a bridge to link together executions over time. Examples of campaigns with bridging longevity that spans decades include Mastercard's 'Priceless' campaigns, Pedigree's use of the colour yellow, Bulmers' use of time as a continuing theme, Red Bull's cartoon style, and red and yellow characters for M&M's. These examples show how a Distinctive Asset can stimulate an ongoing stream of creative ideas. When incorporating Distinctive Assets into advertising, making the most of the qualities that differentiate assets from the brand name can therefore help maximise the value extracted from these assets.

It is important to avoid including assets but leaving them languishing in the fight for attention. If the brand has a colour asset, think about how to make this colour a standout feature; if the brand has a tagline, give it an audio enhancement to improve memorability. Chapters 13 to 17 talk further about how to execute different types of assets, but use the potential of the asset, rather than simply swap out the brand name for the asset.

Assessing the quality of brand execution

One of the key factors holding back brand-execution research, and practice, is the use of the wrong outcome variable. Branding is about making the brand name memorable—nothing more, but also nothing less. Remember the awareness of the brand advertising is one of the necessary conditions for advertising effectiveness.

This objective means the correct branding score is the most useful metric to assess if Distinctive Asset execution is playing its branding role to help build mental availability. Correct branding is a measure of how many people exposed to the marketing activity, preferably in the natural environment, are able to name the brand being advertised. While the absence of the brand is correlated with failure (Hartnett et al., 2016a), the quality of branding execution alone will not guarantee advertising sales success—other factors such as reach, creative quality and messaging also matter. It's like making paella: rice is an essential ingredient for it to work, but rice alone will not make a tasty dish[7].

---

7   While it is possible to make paella using such ingredients as cauliflower instead of rice, I regard this as a sacrilege and will simply pretend such recipes do not exist.

This makes it important to isolate branding objectives from other communications objectives to isolate the impact of branding activities—so branding execution problems can be identified and fixed.

The next chapter explores the role of Distinctive Assets in building another key part of brand equity—*physical availability*.

5

Building Physical Availability with Distinctive Assets

JENNI ROMANIUK AND WILLIAM CARUSO

Mental availability is about making the brand easily thought of in buying situations; *physical availability* its strategic partner in crime. Building physical availability is about making the brand easy to buy, so that mental availability can easily translate into sales. Going back to the Olympics analogy from Chapter 4, if mental availability is qualification for the race, physical availability is the brand's performance on the day: that is, whether the brand is good enough to beat the competition *in that race*.

How Brands Grow: Part 2, Chapter 8, outlines physical availability's three components: *presence*, *prominence* and *relevance* (Nenycz-Thiel, Romaniuk & Sharp, 2016). Distinctive Assets contribute to prominence, in helping the brand get found in its shopping environments. Distinctive Assets that are strong in a shopping environment act like a beacon, drawing a category buyer to the brand through the fog of retail clutter.

The value of a prominent brand in retail environments

In most retail environments, brands battle clutter in efforts to draw category buyers' attention. Distinctive Assets can help a brand stand out in its shopping environments, whether this be within a brick-and-mortar store for a packaged good, signage on a street for a retail brand, or online in the case of an e-commerce store.

When you build a brand's mental availability, you prepare the mind of a category buyer to look for a brand in what is often a chaotic, cluttered environment—think of this as moving the mind of the category buyer closer towards your brand than other brands they have in their brain. Strong shopping assets allow the brand to stand out from other brands, which is like moving your brand closer towards the mind of the category buyer, compared to other brands on shelf. This metaphorical prominence on both sides makes it easier for a category buyer to find, and therefore buy, the brand. This only happens if what is in buyers' minds is a match for what is on shelf—and if what is on shelf for that brand notably differs from competitors.

Figure 5.1: The mind meeting the shelf

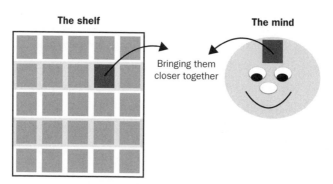

Before talking specifically about Distinctive Assets, we will cover some contextual information on how people shop. This sets the scene for the importance of Distinctive Assets, and which types of assets will be valuable. The focus for this section is on grocery shopping, as this is the context of the majority of relevant research. Other shopping contexts are also very important, but generalised facts are lacking at this stage. We focus on two relevant findings on how people shop for groceries.

Remember the racetrack

While online grocery shopping gains a great deal of hype, a large proportion of shopping still happens in-store. The first important finding we cover is therefore about how people shop in a typical supermarket. It is rare for shoppers to meander up and down every aisle. Instead, shoppers tend to stick to the perimeter of the store (the 'racetrack') and assess each aisle to identify which ones to approach, and to avoid excursions into any aisle perceived as unnecessary to that shopping trip (for example Larson, Bradlow & Fader, 2005). Therefore, a brand benefits from being visible at a distance, as this can trigger the memory of the brand and can remind people of a necessary or desired brand purchase.

Figure 5.2: Racetrack shopper path

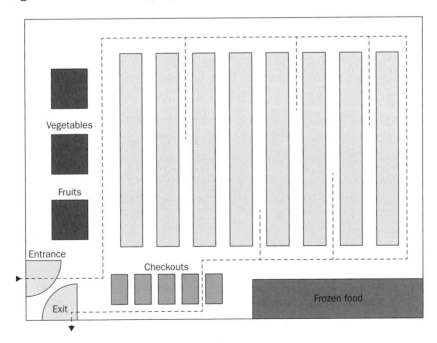

Shoppers shop quickly

It is rare for grocery shopping to involve new or unusual behaviour. A more common scenario is that the buyer draws on years of habitual behaviour when making that specific selection (Sharp, 2010b). Therefore shoppers do not linger in front of shelf or spend time online browsing through different options before purchase, but are able (and want) to make quite quick decisions.

In-store shopper observation studies show shoppers take between 12 and 17 seconds from arriving to leaving a product category. A total of 46% of shoppers take less than 5 seconds to choose an item (Dickson & Sawyer, 1990; Hoyer, 1984; Le Boutillier, Le Boutillier & Neslin, 1994). Likewise, when shopping in an online supermarket, a recent study shows 42% of selections took 10 seconds or less to make (Anesbury et al., 2016).

If one salient brand of chocolate is not available or visible at the time, shoppers have a repertoire of a number of other alternatives (Sharp, Wright & Goodhardt, 2002). This means a brand first needs to have sufficient prominence on shelf to attract the attention of the eye's small field of focal vision (estimated to be around the size of a five-cent piece—Wedel & Pieters, 2006). If it achieves that goal, the brand can be selected. A simple exercise to reveal how much we ignore in shopping environments is to go to a grocery category you buy, in your usual supermarket or hypermarket, or even online store. Pick a category where you don't have any professional involvement to try to be a normal consumer, at least for a moment! Look over all of the options that are available for you to buy. You should find quite a few that you had not previously noticed. In the wide sea of options, it is easy to miss a few things floating around. We don't notice what we don't notice.

The best shopping assets are therefore visible from a distance. Someone should not have to pick up the product to notice the Distinctive Asset.

Distinctive Assets that matter when shopping

Shopping assets are a subset of assets that have particular relevance to the shopping environment. Being easy to find is of premium value in the retail environment, which is cluttered not only with competitors but also other people and objects such as trolleys, which stand between the buyer and the brand. It is also a time when buyers, although engaging in the physical behaviour of shopping, mentally operate with transient, partial attention to the retail environment, with a desire for this shopping to come to a quick conclusion (Dickson & Sawyer, 1990; Nenycz-Thiel et al., 2016; Sorensen et al., 2017).

What makes brands stand out on the shelf

We shop with our eyes, trying to avoid distractions that take time and energy away from our purpose. Visual short cuts help focus attention, but not all visual elements are equal in grabbing attention. In a series of in-store tests, category buyers were asked to identify the brands that stood out on the shelf, and why.

Colour was the most common reason given across brands and categories, irrespective of whether the brand was red, green or any other colour (Gaillard, Sharp & Romaniuk, 2006; Piñero et al., 2010). Figure 5.3 shows the range of responses from Gaillard and colleagues (2006), which highlights the dominance of colour, comprising just over half of responses (52%), with the remaining 48% split across other packaging and placement elements.

A key reason for the power of colour is that it is only thing our eyes can take in when scanning a scene without focusing on anything specific (Wedel & Pieters, 2006). This highlights the importance of developing a colour asset if you can, and protecting any colour assets the brand might have acquired (more on this in Chapter 13).

Figure 5.3: Category buyers' perceptions of elements that make a brand stand out on the shelf

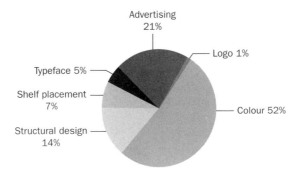

Figures taken from Gaillard et al. (2006)

Challenges to building up strong shopping assets

Shopping assets often fall prey to the assumption from marketers that if something is present (on the pack), it will be noticed. In our experience testing these assets, these are the type with a greater propensity to underperform relative to marketer expectations. The key factors contributing to this gap are lack of innovation, lack of consistency, lack of prominence and lack of distinctiveness.

Lack of innovative thinking about possible assets

A wide range of options could help brands stand out in a shopping environment, but we find the assets marketers put forward for testing are often narrow in scope. The proposed assets often concentrate on colour, shape and logos (later in the chapter we illustrate this by showing the incidence of different packaging assets put forward for testing). This focus on three types of assets leads marketers to miss other opportunities.

This narrow focus on shopping assets also contributes to a flight to the similar, with several brands in the same category trying to build the same type of assets, which increases the risk of competitor overlap. Figure 5.4 outlines a broader set of potential asset types that can be used in a retail

Figure 5.4: The wider set of shopping assets

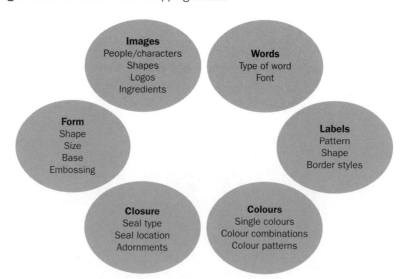

environment, such as shapes, closures, images, labels, words or patterns. While some assets, such as shape, might lend themselves to packaged goods, services and durables also have shopping environments where they need to be found, whether it is in an online store, or down a street cluttered with car yards or coffee shops. Services often also have tangible symbols of the brands like credit cards and ATMs, which can contain Distinctive Assets to make them easy to find[1].

Lack of consistency

Shopping assets get modified in two ways. The first type of modification is the update 'tweak'. Some of these changes are required (for example a change to ingredients); others are often misplaced improvement efforts, such as Tropicana's infamous pack change (Zmunda, 2009).

The second type of modification is the release of limited edition or seasonal designs to attract attention to the brand, such as Orangina's Bikini and Trunk summer pack designs (Tilley, 2017). These short-term possible disruptions to the category can have negative long-term disruptions to category buyers' memory structures for shopping assets. Any such changes need careful consideration to determine if the short-term benefits are greater than the longer-term costs. A particular consideration should be the opportunity cost of the money spent promoting the change that could have been invested in building the brand's Distinctive Assets.

Lack of attention

As discussed in Chapter 4, in advertising and social media, branding has to overcome two challenges to be noticed: distractions in the external environment and distractions within the creative context. Shopping assets face similar challenges. First, these assets have to overcome the external distractions in a cluttered environment of other brands, people and promotional material highlighting special offers. Second, a shopping asset needs to overcome other elements on the pack. For example if the

---

1   Many people have multiple credit cards from multiple banks, and so your bank's credit card competes within the wallet or purse for category buyer attention. The easily found card is likely to be used with greater frequency.

brand has a character on pack as a Distinctive Asset, then this needs to have a sufficient visual presence to be noticed over any health, quality or ingredient signals that might also be on pack.

In a recent study of packaging assets across five categories, Kashmiri, Nguyen and Romaniuk (2017) found that around 40% of Australian packs have a second brand present on pack and one-quarter of these were the same size as the primary brand. All of the clutter on pack makes it difficult for anything to stand out.

It is only when the asset can break through these two barriers that it gets noticed by the shopper.

Lack of distinctiveness

Not all elements of a pack need to be engineered to stand out. Sometimes it is useful to conform to some basic category norms so that the pack is identified as part of the category (Mocanu, 2015; Rosch & Mervis, 1975). But this is only in situations where very clear category codes are present, and the brand should not assimilate so far into the category that it becomes difficult to find.

If a Distinctive Asset choice prioritises category aesthetics at the expense of competitive cut-through, the brand risks becoming lost in a sea of products. It is not that being clearly part of a category is unimportant, but rather consideration of this factor should come after you understand what makes a brand easily found in its shopping environments. In many cases, placement in the retail store signals the category to potential buyers.

The relative performance of shopping assets

Drawing on a database of results from 1001 shopping assets[2] from fifteen packaged goods categories in sixteen countries, we conducted a deeper exploration into the incidence and performance of different shopping-asset types. We wanted to see which shopping assets marketers more often provided for testing in packaged goods categories, and if the assets most often tested are also the assets that performed better than other assets.

---

2   In case you are wondering, yes we did deliberately set a specific goal to achieve more than 1000 assets!

To assess the performance of the assets, we looked at the two key metrics: *Fame*, which is how many category buyers link the brand to the asset; and *Uniqueness*, which is the level of ownership of the asset. Chapters 9 and 10 explain these metrics in detail, but at this stage just know that for both metrics, the higher score the stronger the asset type.

We surveyed a sample of our packaged goods studies, and categorised the packaging assets into one of nine asset types. All asset types related to packaging. That is, colour was only included if it was a colour that was used on the pack, and a character was only included if it appeared on pack.

Figure 5.5 reveals that colour is the most common packaging Distinctive Asset suggested, followed by overall pack design (with only the brand name removed) and the logo. Characters, words and closures were the least common assets provided for testing.

Figure 5.5: Packaging assets provided for testing

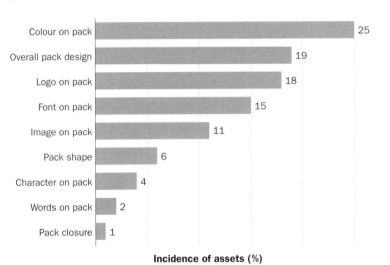

Incidence of assets (%)

It is when we examine the performance of asset types (Figure 5.6) that the common mismatch between how often an asset type is provided for testing, and its performance, relative to other asset types, becomes evident. The most striking difference is for colour, which is the most common asset tested, but performed poorly compared to other types with the lowest average Fame and Uniqueness scores.

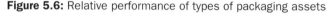

Figure 5.6: Relative performance of types of packaging assets

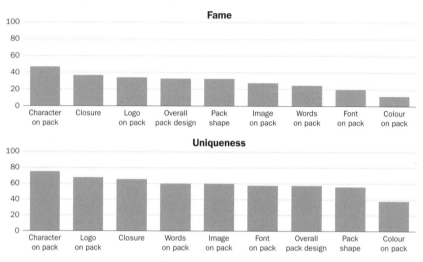

In the other direction, characters on a pack, while only 4% of pack assets tested, have the highest Fame scores of asset types tested, scoring 10 percentage points higher than the next strongest asset type, and the highest average Uniqueness. This is due to a combination of rarity of use, and, as mentioned in Chapter 2, that humans have a natural attraction to faces (Gobbini et al., 2013). Pack closure, such as San Pellegrino's foil covering over the top of the can, is another asset type with a strong performance but is relatively rare in use.

It is not just rarity that gives certain asset types an advantage. A logo is a type of asset that is high in incidence and strong in Uniqueness and Fame performance. This is most likely a result of the combination of logo prominence *and* consistency on packs. You therefore don't just have to seek out the weird, unusual, gimmicky designs for shopping assets: a 'normal' asset that is well executed can still become strong.

As a final point, it is worth noting the low average Fame scores for most packaging assets, with characters on pack, as the strongest, only averaging around 40%. This highlights the (often) large gap between the presence of an asset on pack and the noticing of that same asset. The vast majority of these assets were on the pack at the time of testing[3], yet few

---

3   A few of packaging assets in the data set were from past packs that were tested to see if category buyers still remembered that asset, but this was fewer than 5% of assets tested.

category buyers noticed them. Scores amongst brand buyers were higher, but these still did not reach close to 100%. This reinforces the idea that you can't extrapolate performance from presence, which is why objective measurement matters.

How to improve the execution of shopping assets

Like other Distinctive Assets, the execution of a brand's shopping assets plays a major role in determining their strength. The challenge with shopping assets is that the brand often has only a small amount of visual real estate to work with, in an environment that is largely outside your control. But there are three principles for improving Distinctive Asset execution in this situation.

Embrace the blank space

Sometimes the best tactic to improve the prominence of a particular shopping asset is remove something else from the pack, signage or website. A cluttered background makes it difficult for the asset to stand out. Embracing blank space can help guide the eyes of category buyers towards what you want to be noticed.

Consistency, consistency, consistency

The price of inconsistency of assets in the shopping environment is felt both in buyer memory and the bottom line. Visual inconsistency interrupts the fluency of our recognition processes. If you want to build a shopping asset for a brand, then you need to make that asset visually consistent across all iterations of the brand, including the same assets outside of the shopping environment.

Reach the hard to teach

It is risky to rely on exposure in the shopping environment to build shopping assets, as natural clutter and the distraction of buyers make it difficult to cut through and teach people in that environment. In-store displays and (in some categories) gift packs can help overcome distractions and attract the attention of the brand's non- and light-buyers needed to grow penetration (as shown in Romaniuk, Beal & Uncles, 2013). Again, execution of these in-store devices can play a big role in how much attention is gained. For example Caruso and colleagues (2015) show that end-of-aisle (end-cap) displays reach a greater number of shoppers than in-aisle placement.

A drawback of activities in the shopping environment is that often these need the approval of the retailer to run, which adds to the expense and effort needed. Advertising is another way to build shopping assets amongst non- and very light brand users, and this approach may turn out to be easier, cheaper and offer greater control than in-store activities.

Distinctive Assets in the mobile and e-commerce world

As more people shop online and on mobile phones, a brand's set of shopping assets needs to be able to adapt to the online and mobile retailing environments.

First, let's consider the similarities of different shopping environments. Go to any supermarket online or mobile shopping site, and notice the amount of clutter on the screen. It is just as cluttered as in-store, but with much smaller brand real estate for any specific category. Notice too the abundance of visual special offers and promotional signals that also distract attention. This again reinforces the importance of assets that can attract visual attention, but that have been road-tested to be able to cut through in the presence of distractions online as well as in-store.

Now let's consider the differences. You will notice the clutter online or on a mobile phone screen comprises mainly of words and numbers. This means a great deal of competition for semantic memory, which is where a person's memory for words, numbers and their meanings sit (Tulving, 1972). This reduces the value of words on pack assets, as these are unlikely to be effective when competing for attention.

Another difference is that the initial images are small, which makes it hard to see any detail. To get a bigger image, shoppers need to take the action to click on something, which means they need to first find the brand to click on it. It downplays the value of small or subtle elements like fonts or small ingredient logos, as these qualities are unlikely to be large enough to be noticed. Having an asset that is based on a colour or combination of colours is useful for the brand as these can still attract attention, even when the image is small. But it is important to be mindful that, in this environment, the background colour is often white, and so packs that are white or pale will be at a visual disadvantage.

A third difference in the online shopping world is that there is a greater similarity in the visual playing field across brands. In contrast, on a typical in-store shelf, bigger brands have the advantages of a greater number of facings and these facings sit close together (Nogales & Suarez, 2005). This means in an online shopping environment, if the brand's identity is fragmented across variants, the brand's portfolio will look like a number of small brands rather than one big brand. Further, as there often many subcategories and shoppers can filter the options that appear on screen by functional characteristics (such as gluten free), if the brand's subcategory identifier is greater than the brand identifier, the brand will just look like all of the others in that subcategory.

A final point is that while some Distinctive Assets might work better in an online environment, these same assets need to be a big part of the brand's asset-building activities in the offline world. Most of the reinforcement and building will take place outside of the digital world (that is, in real life). Online buyers still shop in brick-and-mortar supermarkets, and are still trying to find the brand on a physical shelf (Dawes & Nenycz-Thiel, 2014; Nenycz-Thiel & Romaniuk, 2016). While someone might take 17 seconds to buy an item online, that product will sit in the home for a much longer time, impacting the buyer's memory structures each time it is noticed (unless, perhaps, it's chocolate!). Distinctive Assets for an online shopping environment should therefore be a cohesive subset of the brand's Distinctive Assets, not a separate rebel set of assets.

In the next chapter, the roles of Distinctive Assets for sub-brands and category extensions are covered. This chapter also includes handling the tension between resembling the parent brand and the variant having its own separate identity.

6

Extending Distinctive Assets across Sub-brands and Categories

JENNI ROMANIUK

This chapter examines the tension between fitting in with the parent brand identity and a sub-brand (this label also includes variants) or brand extension being identifiable as a separate entity. Remember from Chapter 2, everything presented to category buyers with the same name will get anchored in the same part of memory, and inconsistencies will weaken existing Distinctive Assets. Whenever the brand name is extended into a sub-brand or new category, the question of how much identity overlap will arise as a necessary part of the development process. If the aim for the extension is have a very different brand identity, then it should also have a different brand name. This is to avoid eroding the strength and future potential of the parent brand's identity.

The first step to avoiding a parent–extension clash of identities is to be clear on the actual (or desired) parent brand assets, so you can build or protect these assets.

Protect the parent brand as a priority

The safety demonstration on a plane highlights the importance of self-protection and of putting your own oxygen mask on first, before helping others, even children. A similar self-protection approach should be taken when managing the extension offshoots from a parent brand. Protect the parent brand first and foremost, as a strong parent brand identity benefits everyone, including future extensions.

The first step is to assess the current strength of any parent brand assets, so you can determine their strategic potential for both the parent and any extensions. This is important if the parent brand has already spawned variants, which might have damaged core assets, leaving these assets weaker than expected. I have seen many instances where, despite long-term consistency, the performance of parent assets is weak, because of rampant sub-brand variation in assets. This means it is not possible to assume that long-term use has translated into strong parent Distinctive Assets. As an illustrative example of the extent and type of variation that often occurs with sub-brands or variants, let's take a quick look at Lysol, a common household cleaning brand stocked in Walmart in the USA. Let's compare five variants with the same bottle shape[1], and see how these variants vary from the parent brand and each other, across the dimensions of colours, images, the words on pack, closure and logo/font[2].

Table 6.1 shows the main similarities are the logo, red as a secondary or accent colour, the words 'kills 99% of viruses and bacteria' and the blue closure, except for the Lime and Rust remover variant, which is black. The key areas of difference are in the primary colours, secondary colours,

---

1   The variants selected do not include the other lines in non-bottle packs such as the Automatic toilet-bowl cleaners or other bottles such as the professional range or the bathroom cleaner that also operates under the brand. These variants or extensions tend to display greater variation than the close examples chosen here.

2   As accessed from walmart.com on 17 June 2017.

images, use of white space, and words on the pack. For the pack range to stand out on shelf, the visual power of similarities needs to be greater than the differences. Have a look at the range of visual characteristics: how confident would you be that is the case for Lysol? What could you change to make the brand range stronger in its shelf presence?

Table 6.1: Visual characteristics of Lysol across a subset of variants on walmart.com

	Colours	Images	Words on pack	Closure	Logo font/ colour
Parent: Lysol Power Toilet Bowl Cleaner	Dark blue* **White** **Red** **(accent)**	None	Removes the toughest stains in seconds **Kills 99% of viruses and bacteria**	**Dark blue top**	**Blue cursive font on white background**
Lysol Power & Free	Light blue* **White** Dark blue (base) **Red** **(accent)** Green (accent)	Overlapping OO Bubbles White circular space under logo	**Kills 99% of bacteria** 0% bleach with hydrogen peroxide	**Dark blue top**	**Blue cursive font on white background**
Lysol Power & Fresh Cling Toilet Bowl Cleaner, Country Scent	Light green* **White** Blue **Red** **(accent)** Yellow (accent)	Sunflowers Droplet White circular space under logo	**Kills 99% of viruses and bacteria** Clean & Fresh Thick formula cleans, leaves fresh scent	**Dark blue top**	**Blue cursive font on white background**
Lysol Clean & Fresh Lavender Fields Scent	Purple* White Dark blue (top and font) **Red** **(accent)**	Lavender flowers Droplet White circular space under logo	**Kills 99% of viruses and bacteria** Clean & Fresh Thick formula cleans, leaves fresh scent	**Dark blue top**	**Blue cursive font on white background**

	Colours	Images	Words on pack	Closure	Logo font/colour
Lysol Toilet Bowl Cleaner with Bleach	Dark Green* **White** **Red** **(accent)**	Green swirl Red O with arrows in word 'complete'	**Kills 99% of viruses and bacteria** Max coverage Complete clean	**Dark Blue top**	**Blue cursive font on white background**
Lysol Toilet Bowl Cleaner with Lime and Rust Remover	Black* **White** **Red** **(accent)**	White light (on black background)	Kills 99% of viruses and bacteria Powers through hard water stains	Black top	Blue cursive font on white background

Bolded items are key areas of similarity

*Dominant colour

This discussion is not specific to Lysol; any number of brands could have been used as an example. Lysol just reflects the very common brand architecture for a brand with variants. It also partially explains why, as shown in Chapter 5, it is rare for pack colours to score well for a brand, despite this asset type's popularity and importance. If your brand has variants or sub-brands, it can be eye-opening to do the same exercise and see which dimensions overlap and how many differences exist.

Fixed or optional qualities matter for sub-branding strategy

As well as benchmarking the strength of Parent brand assets, it is also useful to classify current and potential assets based on whether they draw from fixed or optional qualities, as this affects how they can or need to be integrated into sub-brand identities.

- *Fixed qualities*—these are qualities that need to be present in a tangible item, such as colour, font and (for physical items) shape. For example a credit card from a bank has to have a colour, a pack can't exist without a shape and the brand name or text can't be written without a font. While making decisions on these qualities is unavoidable, you do get to decide if you want to make this specific quality one of the brand's Distinctive Assets: while every word written has a font, not every font has to be developed as a Distinctive Asset. However, an asset with a fixed quality, if not used, has to be replaced by a different asset of the same type. For example if the brand has red as an asset, anything that is not red has to be another colour, thus creating the conditions for confusion.

- *Optional qualities*—for these qualities, such as taglines, characters and jingles, you choose whether to include it or not. For example you can decide whether to include a phrase on a pack, or a character in an advertisement. If you don't include that asset, there is no need to have another similar type of asset to replace it. For example if the asset is a tagline, you can omit it from the advertising without needing to put in another tagline.

Parent Distinctive Assets can draw from either fixed or optional qualities. Classifying priority assets as either fixed or optional helps guide Distinctive Asset decisions when extending the brand. The next section discusses two extension conditions: launching a variant or sub-brand in the same category and extending the brand to another category.

Launching a sub-brand or variant

A sub-brand or variant needs to draw on some of the Distinctive Assets of the parent brand, otherwise it is of little value in giving it the parent's name. The question is therefore *which* assets to draw upon, and which assets to ignore or to change or adopt for the variant. Here are some guidelines on how to approach this decision (summarised in Figure 6.1).

Fixed quality means a need for consistency

Parent Distinctive Assets that are embedded in fixed qualities should remain consistent across all incarnations that use that brand name. This consistency serves three purposes:

- it builds a bridge between the parent and the sub-brand
- it increases the total visibility of the parent, thereby increasing its prominence in shopping environments
- it avoids weakening established links for the parent brand in the long term.

Figure 6.1: Making decisions about variant assets

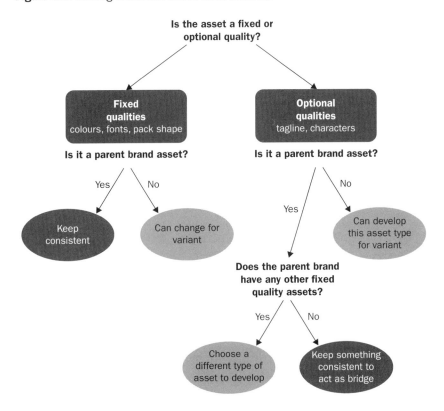

This cohesion across fixed quality assets is of particular importance in situations where the full range is unavailable. For example where distribution is through small 'nano' or convenience stores, common in emerging markets, that rarely stock the full range of any brand; or m (mobile)-commerce, where only a limited number of brands is shown on screen at one time (three is typical). In these situations, the sub-brand needs strong memory links to the parent brand, in the absence of a visual image of the parent brand.

Optional qualities mean choices

You choose whether to use assets that draw on optional qualities. The degree of this flexibility depends on whether the parent brand has fixed quality assets to act as the bridge between the parent and the sub-brand.

If no assets have fixed qualities, then an optional asset needs to become that bridge to the parent brand, and this asset should be kept consistent.

The usual concern is how to signal the sub-brand specifics, or how to distinguish it from the parent brand. It is not always necessary to create a Distinctive Asset to separate the sub-brand from the parent: visible text—for example 'gluten free'—or a simple image signalling the characteristic difference of the variant can also achieve this aim. If the option is expected to be short-lived (for example a seasonal flavour or coinciding with a sporting event such as the Olympics), there is no value in building a Distinctive Asset specifically for that option. Any Distinctive Assets should only be drawn from the parent brand. But if the variant is expected to be around for the long term, it might then be worthwhile considering options for its own Distinctive Assets. This is where the assets with optional qualities can be useful. Many different optional asset types are possible (see Chapter 12 for a comprehensive list) and so the key decision is which type of asset will be most effective for the sub-brand but not damage the parent brand.

Replacing one type of optional asset with something very different within the same type (for example replacing one tagline with another tagline) risks the same confusion and competition issues evident with changes to fixed quality assets, as two taglines become linked to the parent brand. If using the same type of asset is advantageous, due to media or distribution channel benefits, then think about stretching, rather than supplanting, the existing asset. For example if the brand has a character, you can introduce a new family member that shares some characteristics with the existing character. If the brand has a tagline, you could change some words, while keeping others the same. The aim is to keep the total idea cohesive, but carve out a part of the total brand identity to be unique for that variant. But if the available optional assets do not lend to stretching, then chose an asset type unused by the parent brand. This will reduce the risk of mental conflict with the parent brand.

Designing Distinctive Assets for innovations

When designing Distinctive Assets to signal an innovation, whether it be a sub-brand or a new brand, a common trap is to draw on the substance of the innovation to inspire the Distinctive Asset. For example if it is highlighting a natural ingredient, it might incorporate green, a flower, or an image of the earth. The danger is that the additional meaning for the asset makes it attractive for competitors to also draw on the same inspiration when designing their inevitable similar variant. This means that what could have been an asset for the brand becomes a sub-category signal instead.

For example when Coke launched Coke Life, made with a natural sweetener, it came in a green can, which is a common 'natural' colour signal. Pepsi then launched a naturally sweetened product, Pepsi True, in a green can (O'Reilly, 2014). This turned green into a signal for a natural sweetener rather than a potential Distinctive Asset for Coke Life. In a similar vein, Veggie Pret, a vegetarian variant of healthy food chain Pret a Manger, also chose green for its livery. The link between green and vegetarian makes it an obvious choice not only for Pret, but also for any other chain that wants to launch a similar option, while at the same time not building the burgundy colour of the parent brand. In an example in the banking sector, while Citibank uses the colours red, white and blue in its logo, it changes both the name and the colour palette for Citigold, its high-end banking services (for customers with a bank balance of at least $US200,000). Gold is a predictable colour choice for a premium variant, and indeed a quick survey of global banking brands reveals most have a 'gold' variant or sub-brand.

Same, same, but different

The parent brand is the long-term priority, which means the variant should look sufficiently similar that a category buyer unfamiliar with the variant will still be able to notice its parent brand affiliation. In advertising, there should be dual emphasis on the parent brand's Distinctive Assets and the variant signal(s). This enables the variant to contribute in a positive way to the overall mental and physical availability of the parent brand, irrespective of the length of its life.

Distinctive Assets for brand extensions

Launching a brand into a different category only makes sense if it is useful to leverage existing mental structures such as the Distinctive Assets. With strong Distinctive Assets, the brand name and the Distinctive Assets are indistinguishable. Therefore, as with a variant, if you want to give the product in the new category a different brand identity, also give it a different brand name to minimise the risk to the parent brand.

The capacity to leverage past memory structures into a new category is often rooted in overlapping customer bases. The same principles about consistency in assets with fixed qualities therefore apply, to minimise the risk of confusion and competitive interference that will feed back to the parent brand.

The exception to this general rule would be if competitors have substantive links to any of these assets, in which case, it might be necessary to change the extension's focal assets. In this scenario, more than one strong Distinctive Asset is advantageous. For example if your brand has three assets—a colour, a tagline and a logo—and the colour is strong for a competitor in the new category, then you can emphasise the other two Distinctive Assets instead. Again, don't assume competitive Distinctive Asset strength: draw on empirical evidence to avoid making unnecessary modifications to the parent assets.

There are other reasons to adapt your Distinctive Asset–building activities when extending a brand to a new category or country:

- substantively lower asset strength, which means greater initial attention on executions designed for asset building rather than asset using
- different media platforms or distribution channels, which can lead to assets being prioritised or downgraded due to their efficacy in key environments. Sometimes, new asset types will be needed for those new environments.

Adaptation, rather than radical redesign, is still the emphasis. If the parent assets will not work in this new category, then carefully consider using a new brand name instead.

The next chapter examines whether the brand benefits from selecting or prioritising Distinctive Assets that have a strong non–brand name meaning.

7

Does a Distinctive Asset's Meaning Matter?

JENNI ROMANIUK

This chapter is short, but important. It covers one of the major distractions to building a strong brand identity for the long term—trying to select assets with the right, with the strongest meaning.

The many possible options make selecting priority assets a challenge. It can be tempting to use additional criteria, such as a meaning behind the asset, to help in this decision and to try to extract extra value from asset-building activities. This leads to conversations about choosing red to show a brand is vibrant, or a phrase such as 'All natural, All the time' to show the product contains natural ingredients.

The many risks of meanings

It takes time and investment to build a Distinctive Asset. Having asset meaning high on the criteria for asset selection may seem attractive in the short term, but this priority creates issues that could cripple your brand's long-term Distinctive Asset–building. The next section details these issues, and the problems they create.

The risk of picking a fight with heavyweight (mental) competitors

An asset benefits the brand first and foremost because of its connection with the brand name. But the nature of our memory is that the brand is in a constant fight to keep this connection fresh. Other strong non-brand meanings for that asset create mental competition for the brand—and increase the challenges for the brand to overcome in its quest to become, and remain, mentally available (as covered in Chapter 2).

Just think for a moment what having a 'meaning' means from a memory network perspective. Other linked, salient associations define the meaning of anything in memory. This means that if I think I see the moustached man from Pringles and associate him with being Italian, then whenever I see his image in advertising, I have a chance of remembering Pringles, but I also have a chance of thinking of Italy, and then following a mental path to my past trips to Rome, my Italian friends, my favourite pasta and so on. All of these thoughts then compete with Pringles for retrieval from my memory. A richer, more salient, non-brand meaning, results in greater mental competition. This mental competition also interferes with the creation of an asset, the formation of that first asset–brand link, as the brand has to fight its way through a crowded space to become attached to the asset.

These disadvantages quickly negate any possible benefits that an asset rich on non–brand name meanings can bring. But even if the brand is successful, and manages to fight that initial mental competition when establishing the links to the brand name, this can be a short-lived advantage as this fight for retrieval is ongoing if the asset is to remain easy to access in buyers' memories.

The risk of narrowcasting your brand

The use of an asset with strong non–brand name meanings is limited to message contexts where that meaning is relevant. For example if a brand's asset signals 'low prices', such as a 'save' button, then it is only going to be advantageous when the message is about low prices. If the asset's low-price meaning clashes with another message, such as excellent service, the asset turns into a liability.

A solution is to have a greater number of assets, each with different meanings, for use in different situations. But, apart from being inefficient, this doesn't solve the next problem—which is the potential for an expiration date.

The risk of adding an expiration date to an asset

Meanings perceived as attractive for a brand often draw on societal trends—for example health, environment or diversity—thereby allowing the brand to tap into the zeitgeist. But the zeitgeist, by its nature, is transient. Drawing on this changeable phenomenon to develop Distinctive Assets therefore risks spending the resources on developing an asset that then needs to be abandoned as it becomes irrelevant when society changes, as it inevitably does.

Think about the many trends that have come and gone. Food is one area prone to such trends—low fat shifted to low carbohydrate, now the focus is on low sugar. But natural versus artificial sweeteners is also a topic for debate, with concerns being raised, and sugar might come back into favour, similar to how we now should be celebrating 'good fats' in our diet after years of low fats dominating diets and food product innovation. Choosing Distinctive Assets linked to a specific trend gives your brand's assets a shorter shelf life. In contrast, an asset that is defined predominantly by the brand name doesn't become obsolete.

The risk of flocking to the similar

Another risk of choosing an asset because of its non–brand name meaning is that often your competitors are reading the same research and analysis, and therefore likely to come out with something similar. For example with an increased focus on the environment, you might pick assets that also signal environmental awareness—such as the colour green, images of trees or phrases that say how the brand cares for the planet. Remember when there was all this attention on carbon footprint labelling? How long did that trend last? This focus on trends leads to greater risk of overlap and compromises the brand's capacity to own a Distinctive Asset. An example of this is when, during the last financial crisis, most supermarket taglines focused on how they offered low prices. This convergence of ideas meant no single retailer could own this asset.

This is why 'meaning free'[1] is a less risky long-term Distinctive Asset strategy. Yes, competitors still might try to copy the brand's assets but at least the brand will have a head start; the copying is obvious, and therefore has a greater chance of being dealt with in a legal forum.

The prior risks were about a focus on meaning when selecting an asset. The next two are when the perception of negative meaning can lead you to avoid or change an asset.

The risk of 'projection rejection'

It is easy to overthink the meanings of Distinctive Assets. Indeed, much academic research encourages this by asking (and sometimes answering) obscure design questions, such as a recent article in the *Journal of Consumer Research* which examined whether a logo frame is perceived as protecting or confining (Fajardo, Zhang & Tsiros, 2016). This overthinking can lead marketers to reject a perfectly good asset because of a negative meaning that is only projected onto the assets after deep deliberation. Yes, category buyers who think deeply about it may stumble upon the same meaning. But this assumes buyers will both deliberate and come to the same conclusion (as the marketers).

Don't overthink it; buyers won't. Do make sure you have evidence that any meaning you project onto the asset is salient to a considerable number of category buyers *before* you reject an asset on these grounds. This is not to dismiss the value of semiotics research; in the right context, it can be useful, but do make sure any potential negative associations are both present and salient to category buyers.

---

1   This is sometimes referred to as 'meaningless' but this term neglects the most important meaning for the asset, which is the brand name. Strong Distinctive Assets are not meaningless, but rather have the brand name as the primary meaning.

The risk of confusing familiar with stale

Inconsistent use of Distinctive Asset change is encouraged by concerns about established assets being perceived as *boring* or *old fashioned*. A frequent refrain is that the assets are not relevant to millennials. For example the previously mentioned long-term Bulmers advertising theme of 'time' has been dropped for a new idea, considered more relevant to current Bulmers' drinkers, described as aged 18–34 years (Slattery, 2017). In the near future, I am sure we will be hearing how assets need to be changed to ensure they are relevant to Generation Z.

These concerns often come from misguided research, such as asking a small sample of category buyers for their thoughts on assets during in-depth qualitative settings. In these research scenarios, respondents often channel their inner Philippe Starck and become designers, and in the spirit of being helpful, suggest things that should be changed and express complacency about current assets. Many of the benefits that Distinctive Assets have for category buyers are subconscious, and therefore rarely revealed by direct questions into subjective opinions about assets—and group situations are prone to people wanting to feel important.

Consistency is a key factor in building a strong asset and should be celebrated: mentally replace *boring* with *familiar*, and *old fashioned* with *timeless*. This doesn't mean assets need to stay frozen in time. Assets can evolve, but this evolution process needs careful management, as discussed in Chapter 18, not a knee-jerk reaction to misplaced consumer opinion.

How to detect if an asset *does* have a meaning problem

Do you suspect that an asset has non–brand name meanings that interfere with its branding performance? If so, there is an easy test for this issue that involves presenting the asset in a context-free environment and asking a broad, heterogeneous group of category buyers to type in (or say) what comes to mind when they see or hear that asset.

Look through verbatim responses to see if a common singular meaning, which is not the brand name, emerges. If a widely elicited, singular meaning does come forth, the brand may have a problem, and an alternative asset is a safer investment option. The brand wants assets that evoke little (other than the brand name)—the blanker the slate, the easier it will be to make your brand a memorable part of the asset's network for category buyers.

Don't (dis)miss meaning-free opportunities

Being distracted by the meaning of an asset in the selection process can lead you to dismiss (meaning-free) assets that have substantial advantages in building mental and physical availability in favour of other assets that may look like quick, efficient wins but are less flexible or adaptable.

Avoid seeing Distinctive Assets as a short cut to brand image building, as any short-term gains in this are at the expense of an asset's longevity. Distinctive Assets are long-term decisions and making them context-free allows you to keep the brand as the strongest linkage. Context-free assets also have a wider range of situations where they can be applied; their use is not constrained by the advertised message.

If you are concerned about lack of meaning resulting in lack of inspiration, don't be. Evidence from strong assets shows you (or your creative team) don't need to be inspired by meaning to develop or build a strong asset. For example one of the most iconic packaging assets in the world is the Coca-Cola bottle. It was introduced in 1916 and, over 100 years on, still features in Coca-Cola advertising, even though much of the packaging is in other forms. The brief for this was simple, to create 'bottle so distinct that you would recognize it by feel in the dark or lying broken on the ground' (Ryan, 2015).

Another example is the campaign for comparethemarket.com, centred around comparethemeerkat.com, and the character of Aleksandr Orlov and his Russian accent. This idea was developed over a beer at the pub, based on the similarity between the two phrases, and the observation that if you say 'meerkat' with a Russian accent, it sounds even closer to market (Andrews, 2009). No need for a deep analysis into perceptions of Russia or meerkats, and how either relates to insurance.

Remember that assets with no strong meanings are like vacant lots where you can build whatever you want—these assets can become synonymous with the brand much more easily, and this is the gift that can keep on giving for many generations. Rather than be critical of the lack of meaning of a potential asset, celebrate the lower mental competition, lower risk of obsolescence and greater scope for asset usage.

We next move into the section of the book that deals with measurement and metrics, and making smart strategic choices. The first chapter in this section covers the reasons that it is useful to measure Distinctive Asset strength, and the times when this is useful for brand or company strategy.

8

Measuring Distinctive Asset Value

JENNI ROMANIUK

This chapter focuses on the why and when of measuring the value of a brand's Distinctive Assets. It then leads into an expanded discussion on metrics and strategy in Chapters 9 to 11.

Why measurement matters

Why do 93% of US drivers rate themselves as above average (as reported in Svenson, 1981)? It is because, in forming our intuitions, we place greater emphasis on the effects of our own actions and have incomplete or inaccurate information of others' activities. This leads us to overestimate our own abilities, in comparison to everyone else (referred to as the *illusory superiority effect*—Hoorens, 1993). This 'noisy processing' creates errors as we convert our imperfect observations into a judgment (Hilbert, 2012). In a similar vein, how the inputs into your gut feel, when you assess how valuable a particular Distinctive Asset is, is also designed to mislead you.

Subjective judgments on Distinctive Asset value are flawed as they combine biased observations of our own asset-building activities, with an incomplete picture of competitor activities. Our tunnel vision about assets is even more honed, as we tend notice the assets we, ourselves, worked on, over other untouched assets in the portfolio. We also are poor judges of impact, when many of these changes, unless widely advertised, are slow to reach a large proportion of category buyers.

These biases in perceptions inflate brand managers' expectations for certain Distinctive Assets. At the same time they can lead someone to miss the importance category buyers place on other assets, and change something that is important for buyers.

A prime example of this is the mismatch between colour assets provided for testing and the performance results achieved by those same colour assets, as identified in Chapter 5. This highlights the challenge for marketers in trying to use their own instincts to judge the strength of a Distinctive Asset. The only possible way to be confident that a brand owns a specific packaging colour, or any asset in the category, is to measure its strength in the minds of category buyers. Quantitative measures also give objectivity and evidence for Distinctive Asset conversations and decisions.

Why metrics matter

Metrics signal priorities and quantify performance. Therefore metrics should make the end objective clear to all involved, and signpost the path and interim outcomes needed to get to that endgame. Good metrics are also able steer managers away from actions that could (unintentionally) damage the brand in the long term.

Think about designing a pack for a tube of toothpaste. Your aim when designing this pack could be to protect the product inside, in which case the success of that pack is in a low percentage of damaged product, or low spillage level. If you want to design the pack to able to stand out in the toothpaste shopping environment, you need appropriate metrics to know if you have been successful in this endeavour. This is why we need to understand the role of Distinctive Assets: to design the right metrics to assess their strength.

Metrics also provide a common, clear language. Do your colleagues all have consistent definitions for a strong Distinctive Asset? In branding, words such as *iconic*, *strong* and *powerful* are bandied around with little clarity on meaning. Metrics let everyone know the basis for assessments of the strength of a brand's identity.

Appropriate metrics help Distinctive Asset–building by signalling likely problems. While the big mistakes attract considerable publicity, the more insidious issue is the previously mentioned slow death by a thousand cuts that occurs through a myriad of small decisions to change this, and tweak that. Each decision seems inconsequential but the sum of the changes erodes, often unnoticed, the strength of current assets.

For example people often make pack changes in the hope of improving a brand's outcomes, such as attracting buyer attention or highlighting a specific ingredient that will be important to the buyer. But when I poll audiences of marketers about the impact of pack changes, most changes have had a similar (albeit less dramatic) outcome of sales drops. Metrics can help determine if the change is likely to have a demonstrable benefit, and help avoid changes that either have no impact (other than to increase cost) or could damage the brand.

Good metrics are also important catalysts for behaviour. With clear objectives to build the Fame and Uniqueness of an asset, the brand's stakeholders have incentives find opportunities for building Distinctive Assets, rather than treating branding as an afterthought, secondary to the creative idea.

The two metrics that matter

Two metrics, Fame and Uniqueness, integrate knowledge from how memory works, which is where Distinctive Asset associations are stored, and the role Distinctive Assets play in category buyers' lives, which influences how and when we want buyers to use these associations (Romaniuk, 2016b; Romaniuk & Nenycz-Thiel, 2014). These two metrics are defined in these ways:

- *Fame*—quantifies the percentage of category buyers' brains where the brand has a salient link to the asset.
- *Uniqueness*—quantifies the brand's level of ownership of the asset versus competitor brands.

Chapters 9 and 10 give greater detail on Fame and Uniqueness, and how these metrics combine to provide strategic guidance for selecting Distinctive Assets to use and build. The next section covers some other broad, but important, measurement and metric information.

Ignore category norms when setting objectives

A common question is about the objective to aim for in Fame and Uniqueness, and if benchmarks from other similar brands or categories exist that can be used as guidance. At best these category norms are meaningless; at worst they will lead you to 'shoot low' and set suboptimal goals.

Don't limit your Distinctive Asset–building potential—aim for 100% Fame and 100% Uniqueness. This should be the goal of any asset you want to use to replace the brand name[1]. This is achievable, even for smaller brands, if you have the right tactical underpinnings in place.

Does size matter?

Are there natural advantages for big brands when building Distinctive Assets? This question arises because most of the well-known Distinctive Assets are from the big global brands. Past brand experience does underpin most brand equity metrics, and big brands often perform better than smaller brands because of their larger user base (Barnard & Ehrenberg, 1990; Romaniuk, Bogomolova & Dall'Olmo Riley, 2012). Added to this, big brands also often spend more money on advertising (Danenberg et al., 2016; Jones, 1990), which gives them the ability to reach more people with their asset-building activities.

Is there a big-brand bias in Distinctive Asset metrics that would suggest the need to adjust metrics to validly compare across brands? The answer is no: big brands do not always have the most valuable assets, for the following reasons:

- *any sized budget still needs to be spent wisely.* While big brands often spend more on above-the-line activity, this only matters if their

---

1   Romaniuk (2016b) showed examples such as the Apple logo, the Nike 'swoosh' and other assets that score highly on both Fame and Uniqueness.

schedule prioritises reach, so that asset-building activities can have an effect on as many category buyers as possible. Sadly this is still not the case, with much of media spend still reaching a small group of people over and over again.

- *inconsistency.* Big brands often have many people working on marketing activities, which leads to a greater risk of inconsistency.
- *vulnerability to ambition.* Marketers of bigger brands usually find that the easy paths to growth are gone. This leaves changing Distinctive Assets, often without need, as one of the few avenues left for someone to quickly make that splash for promotion.
- *hoarder mentality.* Marketers of big brands often are too ambitious in the number of assets they try to build. This leads to a failure to protect the more valuable assets, making them vulnerable to decay and competitors.

A big brand does have definite advantages of a greater brand-user base, who are likely to notice and screen in asset-building activities, coupled with larger budgets to reach category buyers quickly, but these advantages are often squandered. With greater consistency, smaller brands can therefore gain an edge over bigger brands over time, and this sustained discipline can pay off in the long run.

The right times to measure

An initial benchmarking exercise is the first step to building a strong brand identity. This gives you and your team objective scores on the strength of the current and past brand assets. The results can also guide you about the possible directions the brand's Distinctive Asset strategy could take, which can improve the quality of future decisions.

A benchmarking exercise also compares the brand's performance against competitor brands, something useful to contextualise results. Categories and countries can differ in their level of brand identity maturity, so benchmarking in a few countries, with varying conditions such as different brand shares, media usage, distribution or competitive structure, can be useful to identify consistencies, as well as differences, across countries. This helps you set the strategy for a global brand, and correctly balance local differences with global consistencies.

Other times when it is useful to initiate measurement of Distinctive Assets are grouped into three types of changes: changes to a Distinctive Asset, the brand or the company.

1 Distinctive Asset changes

Measurement is useful for two types of changes to Distinctive Assets: to measure the impact of your efforts, and when someone proposes a major change to the brand's identity.

Assessing the performance of asset-building activities

After a benchmark study, you will have prioritised, and begun, building key assets. When the tactical activities should have reached a substantial proportion of category buyers, the next step is to test the effectiveness of these activities in building buyers' memories. This is important when you start out strategically building Distinctive Assets, to help you move along the learning curve and to understand the efficacy of your efforts, so that you can correct and improve as needed. The timing of this follow-up depends on media weights, but a year is not uncommon if substantive changes to branded material are implemented.

Considering a major change to an existing asset

Pressure to 'freshen up' a brand's identity often coincides with a decline in performance or the emergence of a strong competitor. The brand's identity can also be used as a visible signal of brand's re-energisation to show it is back on track.

This thinking has two problems (first raised in Chapter 1, under the sin of pride). First, it is doubtful that the brand's identity is the primary factor in its sales decline or perceived weakness relative to competitor—so a change in the brand's identity will not fix the problem. Second, change often weakens the brand's Distinctive Assets, which creates a new problem.

But sometimes a desire to change an asset can come from misguided consumer research that asks people how they feel about assets. For example a company wanted to change the brand's colour because respondents in focus groups told them this long-term asset was outdated. Before undertaking any change, it is useful to get the quantitative metrics to highlight the current strength of the asset, and the potential negative impact any change could have. Metrics can improve the implementation of any change by indicating the extent to which direct branding needs increase during the transition to the new asset, or even provide the evidence to avoid unneeded changes to established Distinctive Assets.

2 Brand changes

Brands can change the range offered to existing category buyers or extend out to buyers in a new category. These are riskier and higher investment events and so need to be underpinned by careful planning. In these situations, metrics for the brand's Distinctive Assets can create a platform for the new venture to succeed, while at the same time reducing the risk of the damage to the parent brand's identity.

Adding to the brand's portfolio

As discussed in Chapter 6, a new launch that uses the brand name will affect the parent brand's mental structures. Whether this impact is to the benefit or detriment of the parent brand's Distinctive Assets depends on the successfulness of the integration of these assets into the new launch. A new launch may also introduce potential new assets, and measurement can pre-test these potential new assets for latent competitor linkages, and avoid any risky assets prior to launch.

Extending the brand into a new category

A new category means a new competitive set of brands and Distinctive Assets. For example Snickers in the chocolate category competes against different brands from Snickers in the ice-cream category. It is therefore important to check the brand's Distinctive Assets against these new competitors. Assessing performance in this new context allows you to identify which assets to amplify or minimise. This will help the brand enter the market with the right ingredients to build a strong identity, which leverages its current Distinctive Assets as much as possible.

Extending the brand into a new country

When launching a brand into a new country, again the set of competitors is likely to vary, both in composition and strength. The long-term goal might be to develop global Distinctive Assets but, in the interim, the path may need to adapt to local circumstances. Objective measurement allows you to take the appropriate mix of localisation and globalisation, based on evidence rather than opinion.

Other factors such as media consumption patterns, retail structure and consumer lifestyles may also affect decisions on the best assets to prioritise in a new country. For example there will be a greater emphasis on audio assets in a country where radio consumption is high, while in a country where literacy is low, the value of taglines will also be lower. In countries such as India and Indonesia, where small local stores that only carry small ranges are common shopping outlets, then visible cohesiveness across variants is even more important. In countries like China and South Korea, where e-commerce is rapidly growing, then the priority should be with assets that help in digital and mobile shopping environments.

3 Company changes

These are changes that affect a company's value, such as buying a brand or merging with another company. These events are rare but have a large impact when they occur. Distinctive Asset measurement helps to reduce risk and harvest the most value out of existing brands.

Buying a brand

In brand valuation, much is made about a brand's intangible value, and a brand's identity is a (typically unquantified) part of this. Metrics about the brand's Distinctive Assets allow you to determine if the brand is underusing assets or has the potential to quickly develop a more valuable brand identity.

Company mergers

Corporate mergers are a complicated time for all concerned. Much is made about integration, cost savings, gaining economies of scale and so on. Invariably, as part of this conversation, the issue of each brand's identity arises: what to keep, what to abandon, what to merge and what to create as new.

Mergers are also an emotional time, with most people involved attached to one of the two brands being merged. Distinctive Asset metrics provide objective input into these decisions to avoid any emotion overwhelming good sense, as well as transparency for others who might question any decision. For example if measurement of Distinctive Asset strength reveals one company to have a strong colour in its brand identity, then a case could be made to incorporate this into the new entity's identity. This avoids throwing away the more valuable assets, and reducing the value of the merged company.

The next chapter explores the first key metric for measuring Distinctive Asset strength: Fame.

9

Core Metrics—Fame

JENNI ROMANIUK

This is the first of three chapters that explore metrics for assessing Distinctive Asset strength. It focuses on Fame, which is how well known the asset is amongst category buyers. Over time Fame scores reflect the success of efforts to keep fresh or strengthen links between an asset and the brand name.

Building Fame: the shift from risk to value

Building Distinctive Assets means creating proxies for the brand name. The word *Nike* means Nike, but for many people, so do the phrase 'Just do it' and the 'swoosh' image. A Distinctive Asset's Fame score dictates its value as a brand proxy: the higher the score, the greater the value of the asset; the lower the score, the higher the risk associated with using that asset as a stand-alone branding device.

Using the brand name is 100% effective in that anyone who notices the brand name takes away the intended brand name meaning[1]. If I see HSBC written or hear it spoken somewhere, I know the advertisement

---

1 The underlying assumption is that the brand name and broad category offering are known to category buyers. If prompted brand awareness is low, such that people do not even know what the brand offers, then this needs to be addressed before Distinctive Assets are developed.

or speaker are referring to HSBC. But if I see a print advertisement with a red border, I also think of HSBC, because I have this link 'red border = HSBC' established in my memory.

Suppose I am with my niece, Gabby, who does not have that 'red border = HSBC' link in her memory. She sees the same advertisements but all she registers are pictures with red borders. Unless she also notices the HSBC brand name in the advertisement, the advertising exposure is of little value to HSBC. Any emotion or message becomes filed generically in her memory, rather than in the HSBC part of her brain.

For HSBC, a large part of the value of the red borders as a branding asset depends on how many people resemble Gabby or me. The more the category buyers resemble me, the more valuable the asset as a branding device. The more the category buyers are like Gabby, the greater the risk associated with using the asset as a branding device, and the more prominent the brand name needs to be to ensure the Gabbys of the world file the exposure correctly in the HSBC part of their memory network.

Fame, as a metric for Distinctive Asset strength, is therefore quantified as how many of the people you are trying to influence (often category buyers, but sometimes the audience is larger) link your brand to the asset. Knowing this score guides appropriate use of assets, and mitigates the risk associated with assets with lower Fame. A weaker asset need not be abandoned, but can be built up with execution techniques to connect the asset to the brand name amongst a wider cohort of category buyers. But this building of an asset will only happen with a deliberate decision to include the brand name or when another asset is also present to anchor the exposure. Without the low Fame scores to justify this decision to include the brand name, effective anchoring is unlikely and Fame scores will remain low.

An unused asset will also drop in Fame. As memory decays, the strength of the link erodes in memory and the brand is less often retrieved. A decline in Fame scores therefore reflects asset neglect—either lack of use or poor execution efforts with insufficient cut-through to have an impact on category buyers.

Achieving 100% (or close) Fame is the goal, and is possible. As you will see in Chapters 13 to 17, any type of asset can reach this 100% target.

Measuring Fame

In a paper published in the *Journal of Advertising Research*, Magda Nencyz-Thiel and I tested four approaches to measuring Distinctive Asset strength. The approaches had varied cues (the brand or the asset) and response types (unprompted or prompted). Our results show that the combination of using the asset as the cue and collecting brand names unprompted is the best approach (Romaniuk & Nencyz-Thiel, 2014).

This asset cued–brand unprompted measurement approach also replicates the desired role for Distinctive Assets: to trigger the brand, in the brand's absence. This is a very important point. While methods that prompt for brands are easier on respondents, these approaches are prone to false positives or guessing that inflates scores. By providing the brand, prompting for brand names also fails a face validity test—that assets are able to trigger the brand when the brand is *not* present.

We are able to measure Distinctive Asset strength with a well-constructed survey that takes into account how our memory works, as well as its limitations, such as proneness to priming, where one response can make another more likely than normal. While other more complicated methods might be employed, such as measuring via implicit approaches, for example response latencies, these approaches do need to add substantive value to justify the additional expense needed to get a full category assessment. I have yet to see the evidence these approaches are worth the additional effort and expense. Most of the approaches I have seen also fail to capture linkages to competitor brands, which make it difficult to assess Uniqueness levels.

Common patterns in Fame scores across customer segments

Testing for segment differences to identify where customers score higher or lower is a typical market research exercise. You discover if the brand's performance is stronger amongst 18–24-year-olds, weaker amongst men and so on. In Distinctive Asset measurement, testing for segment differences in Fame scores can also be useful. These common patterns can help you to understand how well your brand's asset-building activities are working, or if an asset has been neglected.

There are a few twists in the interpretation. Segment differences often reflect shortfalls in performance rather than success stories, and so the absence of segment differences is a positive result. It suggests no biases in your media or creative executions. If there exist significant differences in asset Fame for age, gender or brand usage, the results may follow one of the following patterns.

Age

When it comes differences in Distinctive Assets across age groups, three consistent patterns pop up with relative frequency (see Figure 9.1):

- *The neglected asset*—this is when the Fame scores rise with the age of category buyers. This asset has either not been used or has been poorly executed in recent campaigns. To remedy this situation, either fix the execution issues or start using the asset. Reviewing past execution successes can be useful to address this problem, particularly if changes have been made in how the asset is executed.
- *The Snapchat-heavy asset*—this is when Fame scores decline as category buyers age. The typical cause of this pattern is media scheduling that overemphasises younger category buyers, and has failed to refresh the asset amongst older category buyers. To remedy this situation, review media plans and asset-building activities, and change activities to reach all category buyers. For example if you invest in media skewing to younger category buyers, counterbalance this with media that reaches older category buyers as well.
- *The shopper asset*—this is when a Fame score bump amongst females aged 25–50 years is evident; this often reflects a media spend focused on the household shopper demographic, rather than all category buyers. Building assets amongst this group is not a liability, as long as the neglect of other category buyers is remedied.

Gender

Gender skews can originate from creative or media biases. An example of a creative bias is when 30% of category buyers are males but the brand's advertising never features men using the product. This could lead males to switch off, meaning they do not get exposed to the brand's asset-building activities. If the asset has significant gender bias, then check each gender's reaction to the creative execution that uses the asset.

Figure 9.1: Examples of Fame distribution patterns across category buyers' ages

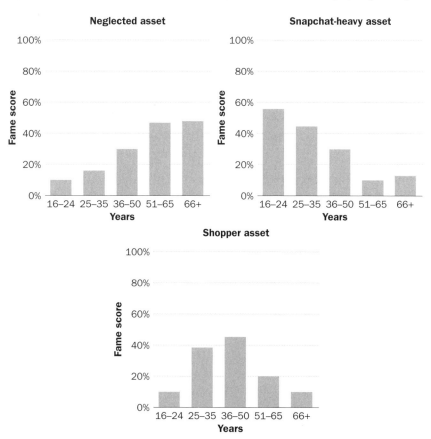

Media planning can also create gender biases. For example advertising in a predominantly male sports events when the brand is a male razor brand might seem logical, but this can mean your brand's asset-building activities don't reach the many female shoppers who buy razors for their male partners or teenage sons. There might also be an issue with the weight of media, such as hitting men ten times with asset-building activities, but women only once, which can also cause an imbalance in Fame metrics.

Brand users

More valuable Distinctive Assets have fresh links to the brand name for both brand users and non-users. A brand's asset can't get to more than 80% Fame without educating non-users. Advertising is one of the primary mechanisms to reach and build assets amongst non-users, subject to the brand name being employed as an effective anchor.

If an advertising asset's Fame scores are low amongst non-users, this suggests a prominence or anchoring problem in advertising execution. That is, either the asset is not noticed or it is not co-presented with the brand name. If a packaging asset scores lower in Fame amongst non-users, this suggests that reinforcement is most often occurring in the shopping environment, and it would be advantageous to place emphasis on building the asset in wide-reaching advertising activities. If the packaging asset is already used in advertising activities but is still weaker amongst non-users, this also suggests an anchoring or prominence issue.

The partial exception to this rule about no difference between brand users and non-users is in *dark* markets, where advertising is prohibited for that category (for example alcohol in India). In dark categories, a difference between brand users and non-users should be expected for lower Fame assets, and should only be of concern if the differential for a particular asset is disproportionately large. In these markets, the user base of the bigger brand does provide an advantage in building valuable Distinctive Assets, but with the cluttered shopping environment as the main source of asset-building activities, building assets will be a challenge for all brands.

Fame is the first step toward a valuable Distinctive Asset, but it is of little value without Uniqueness, which is the subject of the next chapter.

10

Core Metrics— Uniqueness

JENNI ROMANIUK AND ELLA WARD

This chapter covers Uniqueness, the second core metric to help assess the strength of a Distinctive Asset. Uniqueness measures the brand's level of asset ownership and should be 100%, which means that the asset triggers only one brand in memory. A lack of Uniqueness means the asset can trigger competitor brands alongside, or instead of, your brand.

In this chapter we further explore the area of mental competition (which was first introduced in Chapter 2), the antithesis of Uniqueness. We discuss different models of mental competition, the scenarios where asset Uniqueness tends to be low, and provide suggestions about how to tackle these situations.

The value of Uniqueness

Uniqueness has long been appreciated as a valuable quality for brand associations (for example see Keller, 1993). For Distinctive Assets, Uniqueness is crucial to build mental or physical availability. For example when building mental availability, if the brand is uniquely linked to the asset, a *category entry point* (CEP) link is freshened for your brand and only your brand. In contrast, if the link to the asset lacks Uniqueness, the benefit of reaching the category buyer and refreshing the CEP is either cancelled out (if a competitor is retrieved alongside the brand) or counter-effective if only a competitor is retrieved.

Lack of Uniqueness also affects an asset's contribution to physical availability. If an asset is attributed to multiple brands, it may lead people to find a competitor instead of your brand if, say, they are looking for 'the blue one', and multiple blue options exist. This is risky in an environment where the brand's competitors are present and, if noticed, could also be bought.

Measuring Uniqueness provides an assessment of the level of mental competition the brand faces from other brands in the category, and the nature of this competition. Mental competition is competition within the mind for retrieval, just as sales competition is competition in the store for revenue. Two brands from the same company (for example Pantene and Aussie, both owned by Procter & Gamble) attached to the same asset can still compete mentally, even if the revenue goes back to Procter & Gamble irrespective of the brand bought. While mental competition between two brands from the same company might not affect short-term revenue, the confusion and retrieval interference can affect the capacity of either brand to compete in the wider category, and hamper the portfolio in the long term.

Calculating Uniqueness scores

Chapters 8 and 9 covered data-collection approaches. Uniqueness is calculated from that same data, as the share of *responses* the brand gets among competitor brands. This makes it important that any questionnaire used is designed to encourage respondents to give multiple responses when several brands are salient and to capture those responses without descending into a brand-recall guessing game. It is also necessary to avoid inhibition, where a response to one question dampens the response to the next questions, as this can stifle mention of a competitor brand and lead to overestimation of an asset's Uniqueness.

Uniqueness can range from 0% (not linked at all) to a 100% share of responses (the only brand mentioned). If a brand's Uniqueness is under 50% for a given asset, competitor brands dominate responses, making the asset risky to use. If Uniqueness is over 50%, then the brand dominates the responses and the risk is lower, with the risk continuing to lower as Uniqueness moves closer to 100%.

Table 10.1: Examples of Uniqueness calculations

Possible response options from 100 respondents	Brand responses (*n*)	Competitors responses (*n*)	Calculation	Uniqueness (%)
Scenario 1	50	20	50/(50 + 20)	71
Scenario 2	50	100	50/(50 + 100)	33
Scenario 3	50	40	50/(50 + 40)	55

Table 10.1 illustrates different examples of Uniqueness calculations. Remember: respondents can name one or more brands, or not even name any brands, so the total number of brand responses does not need to add up to the sample size. Total brand responses can be lower than the sample size if people have few or no brands linked to the asset; or they can be higher than the sample size if many people have multiple brands linked to the asset.

Are some asset types prone to greater or lower Uniqueness?

We collated different asset types to see if some generally exhibit higher or lower Uniqueness. The aim was to highlight any particular asset types with greater or lower vulnerability, which can feed into decisions about which asset types to develop.

Across 1512 assets, from thirteen packaged goods categories, Ward (2017) found that characters, logos and fonts are, on average, the most unique asset types (see Figure 10.1). Category buyers' memories are likely to hold only one brand for these asset types.

At the other end of the scale, colours and advertising styles are significantly less unique when compared to other asset types[1]. With average Uniqueness less than 50%, these assets are typically shared amongst competing brands more often than they are uniquely owned by a single brand. A further six types, such as advertising moments, taglines,

---

1   For colour, this extends the results found for colour packaging assets in Chapter 5 to other colour assets.

product forms and images on pack, were also tested but no significantly higher or lower Uniqueness scores were evident.

Although the results indicate that some asset types typically have a Uniqueness advantage or disadvantage, results varied widely within each asset type. This variance within asset type suggests that selection and execution play an important role in a brand's level of ownership. Even assets such as colour and advertising style with lower Uniqueness still have individual assets that are highly unique. Likewise, while characters generally scored higher on Uniqueness, there are still some highly competitive character assets with low Uniqueness. Later chapters delve deeper into the performance of different assets.

Figure 10.1: Relative Uniqueness by asset types

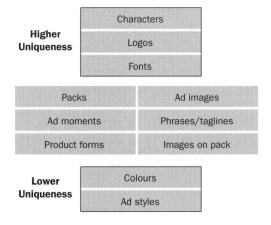

Sources of mental competition

Mental competition originates from two sources: genuine exposure to multiple brands using the same or similar assets; or false attribution, where two people see the same exposure but one confuses the brand with that of a competitor.

Real exposures can be due to competitors mimicking assets, the use of category or subcategory codes, functional qualities of innovations, or an unfortunate consequence of drawing on assets that signal consumer trends, resulting in a flight to the similar (as covered in Chapter 6). These scenarios set up the situation for multiple brands to compete for retrieval for the same asset.

One of the benefits of measuring Uniqueness is the capacity to examine the structure of competitive responses, and distinguish between the two main types of mental competition.

Two types of mental competition

When Uniqueness is 100%, only the target brand is linked to the asset for all category buyers who have a brand link (see Figure 10.2). But low Uniqueness can be due to two different types of mental competition, which we refer to as the *Battle for Brains* and the *Battle for First Spot*.

Figure 10.2: Types of mental competition

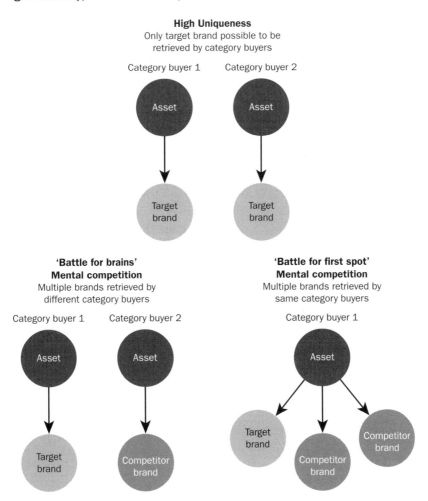

- *'Battle for Brains' mental competition*—this is where category buyers tend to have only one brand linked to the asset, but this brand differs across people. For example the asset triggers Brand X for Category Buyer A, and Brand Y and for Category Buyer B. In this instance, the battle is to gather as many brains as possible, before your competitors do, and hope that your competitors give up promoting this asset and surrender the mental territory to your brand.
- *'Battle for First Spot' mental competition*—this is where exposure to the asset triggers multiple brands in a single category buyer. For example an asset triggers Brand X and Y in Category Buyer A. In this instance, the battle is to be fresher in memory than a competitor's brand.

Both of these mental competition models are possible—but does either tend to dominate?

The competitive structure of brand–asset links

A score of 50% Uniqueness may result from fifty people recalling the same single brand, and another fifty people recalling another brand (Battle for Brains), or a group of fifty people who say two brands while the remaining fifty people recall nothing (Battle for First Spot). Therefore Ward (2017) took a subset of greater than 1000 Distinctive Assets, where the lead brand had less than 80% Uniqueness, to investigate whether category buyers typically respond with a single brand or multiple brands.

She found that of the two possible types of mental competition, if Uniqueness is lacking, then the 'Battle for Brains'–level mental competition prevails. That is, when Uniqueness is low, category buyers tend to have only one brand linked to the asset, but that brand differs across people. Across all assets with Uniqueness lower than 80%, 93% of people gave a single brand response. This figure ranged from 96% for logos to 90% for the asset types with the lowest average Uniqueness, colour and advertising style. As the brand that consumers remember each time varies from individual to individual, a key factor in the capacity to build the asset Uniqueness is how many 'free' brains, without any brands linked to the asset, are available. The greater the number of free brains, the greater your capacity to remedy lower Uniqueness.

Building Uniqueness and combating mental competition

Overcoming mental competition and building Uniqueness are more challenging than building Fame, because you can't tell category buyers to 'unthink' something or stop competitors from advertising a similar asset[2]. You can only hope that, over time, competitive links become sufficiently weak such that the memories fall below the retrieval threshold (as per Collins & Loftus, 1975).

Perhaps you want to develop an asset that does currently suffer from low Uniqueness—what now? In this scenario, the way forward depends on the distribution of the responses for competitors' brands. If responses are fragmented over multiple brands, then mental competition is not well established, and could be overcome with smart execution.

To further explore the structure of brand responses under conditions of varying levels of Uniqueness, we examined four multi-country studies measuring Distinctive Assets for different categories. In each category, we first quantified how many assets had a lead brand with more than 70%[3] Uniqueness. As shown in Figure 10.3, this is the most common outcome, ranging from 67% for the snack category to 34% in the alcohol category. Categories can therefore vary a great deal in the number of highly unique assets. We then quantified the proportion of assets that had a brand with less than 70% Uniqueness, but with no other brands competing for that asset, as indicated by scoring over 10% of responses[4]. This turned out to be the smallest group of assets, ranging from 2% in the food category to 7% in the alcohol category.

For the remaining assets where Uniqueness was lower than 70%, we determined how the remaining brand responses were concentrated: in one competing brand; across a small set of competing brands; or dispersed across many different brands. The results show this was evenly split between a single competing brand and multiple competing brands, suggesting both scenarios have an equal likelihood. This tells us that the

---

2   Legal options are possible, but these are expensive, and rarely successful.
3   If Uniqueness is more than 70% there is little chance of any other brand reaching more than 10% of responses.
4   A brand was considered as competing on that asset if it achieved more than 10% of responses for that asset.

Figure 10.3: The nature of brand competition

■ >70% Uniqueness ■ <70% Uniqueness, no single brand competition
<70% Uniqueness, one brand competing ■ <70% Uniqueness, multiple brands competing

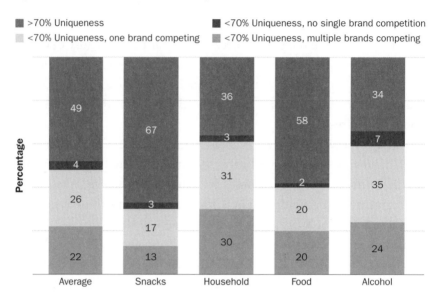

majority of cases of lower Uniqueness are due to direct competition from one or more competitors, rather than confusion.

Benchmarking Uniqueness scores for different brand competition structures

We can use this analysis to highlight benchmarks where a competitor brand should be of particular interest. Let's consider the brand that gained the most responses for an asset as the primary brand. The average Uniqueness of the primary brand declines predictably as a greater number of competitor brands score over the 10% response threshold, from 63% (if there are no competitors with more than 10%) to 29% if four competitor brands score greater than 10% (see Figure 10.4).

Unlike the primary brand's Uniqueness scores, the Uniqueness score for the second brand varies little, ranging from 23% to 20% across the two, three and four competitive brand scenarios. This score can therefore be used as a benchmark to identify when the nearest competitor has an unusually high score on an asset (for example 30% Uniqueness) or unusually low (for example 10% Uniqueness). A higher-than-average

Figure 10.4: Uniqueness scores for brands (across 19 studies in four categories)

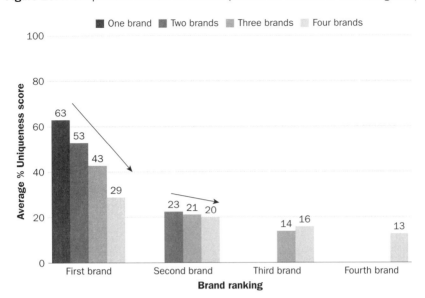

score suggests a well-entrenched competitor, and this means overcoming the lack of Uniqueness will be more difficult.

The conditions conducive to reclaiming Uniqueness

An asset's Uniqueness is influenced, but not determined, by asset type. Selecting a character, logo or font provides an advantage for building a unique asset, but this is not a fail-safe guarantee for brands.

A deeper understanding of what lower Uniqueness looks like in category buyers' memories helps us work out the viability of different paths to address Uniqueness challenges. The results suggest it is useful to look out for two signs:

- the number of 'free brains' available: the greater the number of free brains, the higher the potential for the asset to be rehabilitated
- the competitive structure—if the second brand has more than 20% Uniqueness, this will be a harder task to overcome than if there are no brands with more than 20% Uniqueness.

Given the wide number of potential options for Distinctive Assets, if the asset doesn't have many free brains or a competitor has already made major inroads into that asset, we suggest it would be prudent to instead prioritise an alternative asset.

The next chapter shows how the two metrics of Fame and Uniqueness combine to provide strategic guidance about an asset's development potential.

11

Setting a Distinctive Asset-building Strategy

JENNI ROMANIUK

This chapter shows how the two metrics of Fame and Uniqueness can combine to create the *Distinctive Asset grid* (Romaniuk, 2016b). Positions on the grid indicate each asset's potential, and examining this potential across all assets can highlight strategic directions for a brand's overall identity. The implications of assets placed in each of the four quadrants, as well as how to interpret some common grid patterns, are also covered.

The Distinctive Asset grid

A valuable Distinctive Asset needs both Fame and Uniqueness, with a target of 100% Fame and 100% Uniqueness. This is when the asset is of most value—and synonymous with the brand name. Most potential assets are not at that target point, often with several partially developed assets available, a greater number than resources can cover. The Distinctive Asset grid can help identify which assets provide best opportunities to develop.

The Distinctive Asset grid consists of four quadrants, all separated at 50%. This cut-off signals when the odds are in the brand's favour. If a brand has over 50% Fame, then a category buyer is more likely than not to think of the brand when exposed to the asset. If a brand has over 50% Uniqueness, then that brand dominates the responses for that asset.

Figure 11.1: The Distinctive Asset grid

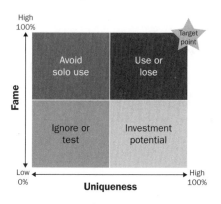

From Romaniuk (2016b)

The *use or lose* quadrant

If the brand has assets placed in this quadrant then congratulations, particularly if you followed the measurement approach recommended in Romaniuk and Nenycz-Thiel (2014), which is deliberately a difficult, risk-averse measure. If the asset is in the top-right corner of the quadrant, with close to 100% Fame and 100% Uniqueness, then it *can* be used as a replacement for the brand name. Indeed the asset *needs to be used* if you want to retain value, which is why the quadrant is called *use or lose*. Remember the natural state of memory is to decay, and so category buyers need to be exposed to the asset to keep it fresh. While Uniqueness will only change if competitors start to compete for your brand's asset, any asset will decline in Fame over time if neglected.

If an asset just sneaked into the quadrant (say 55% Fame, 80% Uniqueness), then your asset-building work is not complete. A sizeable proportion of the market does not link the brand to the asset, and your marketing activities need to reach and educate these category buyers. This means it is necessary to include brand–asset co-presentation moments to widen and strengthen the links with the brand name. It is also prudent to look for category-buyer segments that lag in Fame scores (see Chapter 9), as this can help identify any shortfalls in execution or media planning that are hampering asset building.

For all assets, even the most valuable, you need to be mindful of new category buyers, who still need to learn about the brand's Distinctive Assets. In a growing category this is important but even in mature categories the category user base still churns (people die, people are born, people have life changes like having children). Where possible, have activities aimed at building assets amongst these new category buyers. For example pay particular attention to asset-building activities for any entry-level portfolio option that tends to attract a disproportionate amount of new category buyers.

Key performance indicators for assets in this quadrant should capture two important objectives: maintenance of metrics for valuable assets, and the successful building of assets amongst newer category buyers.

The *investment potential* quadrant

Some Distinctive Assets gain the majority of responses (greater than 50% Uniqueness), but only amongst a minority of category buyers (less than 50% Fame). This type of asset is classified as having *investment potential* because the high Uniqueness score gives the brand a head start in building the asset and because Fame is easier to build than Uniqueness. You control your brand asset's Fame-building activities via the reach and quality of execution, while your control over Uniqueness is often lower and depends on competitors' activity.

Assets that have been around for a while, but sit in the investment-potential quadrant, have often had one or more of these characteristics:

- used sporadically, so asset–brand links have been weakened by memory decay
- often changed, so each exposure has not reinforced the same asset–brand link
- lacked prominent execution, so asset-building activities have passed by unnoticed.

These issues that hold back Fame can usually be fixed with greater attention to consistent, widespread and prominent asset-building activities.

But the *potential* part of *investment potential* also means just because you could doesn't mean you should. The benchmarking process, where a wide range of assets is tested, typically produces a greater number of assets in this quadrant than can be properly resourced. This makes it necessary to identify assets that are priorities for investment.

There are several steps to help in the prioritisation process.

Step 1

The first step is to rule out any assets that will add further difficulty to an already challenging task. If assets you are considering have lower than 70% Uniqueness score, look in detail at the responses for competitors' brands. If another brand is a major mental competitor for that asset (as discussed in Chapter 10), then this asset should be a lower priority.

Step 2

The next step is to look at the Fame scores in this quadrant, and prioritise assets with higher Fame. In this quadrant, Fame scores can vary from 1% to 49%, and an asset with 40% Fame has a considerable head start over one with less than 10% Fame.

Step 3

The third step is to revisit the roles of assets, and examine each of the remaining assets through the lens of the following questions:

- *How can it be used to build physical availability?* Assets that help the brand stand out in its retailing environment are of particular value.
- *How can it be used to build mental availability?* Assets that can help you better execute branding in marketing communications are beneficial.
- *Will it add neurological diversity?* Assets that reach out to a new part of the brain have greater value, as you widen the neurological potential of the brand's Distinctive Assets.

If an asset can check all three boxes, then it is a good choice for prioritisation.

One usable asset is better than ten investable ones, so prioritise one or two assets for the short term, before expanding the priority list to other assets. This might mean sacrificing something with potential to ensure asset-building activities are focused on creating those one or two priority assets. The benefit of this focus is that, once your brand has a valuable asset, this asset helps make it easier to build the next generation of assets, as it gives you another anchor for future asset-building activities. For example if your brand develops a logo asset, a spokesperson could wear this logo to build linkage between that person and the brand name.

The *avoid solo use* quadrant

An asset in this quadrant should be of concern as it means category buyers link it to your brand *and* to those of competitors. The circumstances where this occurs include the following:

- an asset that has become a category indicator, such as red and green as category colours for pasta sauce
- an asset that signals a functional variant, that is then copied by competitors to provide a mental short cut as to the nature of the variant, such as pink for fish variants in cat food
- a competitor has directly copied an asset: for example when a private label mimics the category leader or, in emerging markets, local competitors copy successful elements from foreign brands.

Relying on assets in this quadrant as either branding devices or cues to find a brand gives the brand's competitors mental real estate. This is never beneficial. Remember: for category buyers, many of whom also use competitor brands, the mental availability of a competitor might be stronger than the brand. The best outcome is the brand is retrieved alongside competitors, while the worst outcome is only the competitor is evoked, which is like donating your media budget to your competitors. If using the asset is unavoidable, then accompany the asset with strong direct branding to avoid wasting your marketing budget.

How to reduce the chance of an asset moving into the avoid solo use *quadrant*

These steps can help minimise the chance an asset will fall or move into the *avoid solo use* quadrant:

- Avoid trying to develop category codes into brand assets. If you have to use the same pack shape as every other brand, then don't try to build this into an asset.
- Make sure variant assets are linked to the variant brand only, and not signalling a functional quality.
- Have a system to monitor competitors' use of assets, and metrics able to quickly pick up declines in Uniqueness.

Is it useful to deliberately target a competitor's asset?

It is risky to try to capitalise on a competitor's asset. The most obvious risk is that of losing the mental competition battle and simply strengthening the competitor's asset. A less obvious risk is the opportunity cost. While trying to tear down competitors, the brand misses the opportunity to build Distinctive Assets with their own Fame and Uniqueness.

The *ignore or test* quadrant

Assets in this quadrant fail to reach the majority of responses in both Fame and Uniqueness. Potential new assets typically fall into this quadrant, but this does not mean it is necessary to reject the new asset. The purpose of testing yet-to-be-introduced assets is to double check whether competitors already have existing traction on that asset, which will hamper efforts to build this new asset.

Presence in this quadrant is a negative result if there have been prior efforts to build an asset. It suggests these prior efforts have been ineffectual. In this situation, unless you can make dramatic changes to your execution tactics, it is time to move your focus to another asset.

It is also important to remember that if something you tested is placed in this quadrant, this is only an assessment of its branding potential. You may still use it in advertising or on pack if it has useful messaging properties, or it helps you evoke a desired emotion (assuming there are no strong links to competitor brands). Just recognise that this element is not acting as an effective brand signal, and include other devices to communicate the brand.

How to interpret common Distinctive Asset–grid structures

After years of testing across brands, categories and countries, some common grid structures have emerged (see Figure 11.2). This section describes these structures, and gives some suggestions about how to handle each scenario.

Figure 11.2: Common grid structures

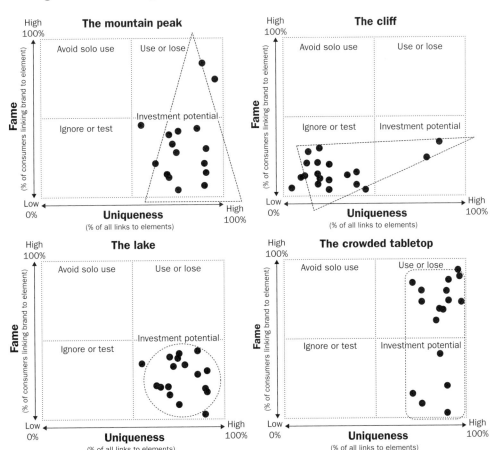

The mountain peak

The mountain peak is characterised by one or two usable assets, and many investable assets.

If a brand's Distinctive Assets follow the mountain peak structure, then the brand has one or two valuable Distinctive Assets, and this is a good place to be. If these assets are lower in the *use or lose* quadrant, then the first priority is to build these assets further and have them reach 100% Fame and 100% Uniqueness.

The next step is to widen the platform of usable assets, and diversify into other asset types. Consider the types of assets the brand doesn't have, media platforms used to build assets and the channels where the brand is sold, and use these factors to prioritise one or two *different but useful* investable assets as the next tranche to build. For example if the brand has a strong tagline, then a visual asset can be a useful complement. If you have a strong logo, then a character or a tagline might be good next options. Or if the brand has two visual assets, and uses media with an audio component, then an audio asset could be a good next step. If none of your brand's usable assets are shopping Distinctive Assets, then this can be a useful type to add. The aim is to achieve useful diversification.

The cliff

The cliff structure is characterised by one or two investable assets, and many assets in the *ignore or test* quadrant.

This is a sideways version of the Mountain Peak, and has similar recommendations, except much more work is needed to turn investable assets into usable ones. Brands with one or two investable assets have a good starting point but, given these assets are still only at *investment potential* level, it is worthwhile assessing the quality of the assets before making the final decision to prioritise.

Sometimes an asset with greater *investment potential* at this point in time may be dropped in favour of a lower-performing asset that has greater promise for building mental and physical availability in the long term. For example with this grid formation, the font is the single investable asset, because this has been the only asset used often, with consistency. This asset, however, might not be the best long-term investment choice—a different asset with greater creative potential might be a smarter investment decision.

The lake

The lake is characterised by no usable assets, but many with investment potential.

The lake grid structure is when the assets pool together in the *investment potential* quadrant. This can be symptomatic of brands that have lacked a strategic plan. It is characterised by a number of different efforts at building assets, but none with sufficient perseverance for the asset to gain traction with the majority of category buyers. The media strategy can also be at fault, because if a reach-based strategy is not employed, then large segments of category buyers are likely to remain untouched by all asset-building activities.

Prioritising assets is the primary goal to get strategy back on track. The first step is to group the assets into types, so similar assets can be assessed against each other to detect any clear winners. For example you may have tested two different taglines, and one might have 45% Fame and 80% Uniqueness, while another tagline asset might have only 10% Fame and 56% Uniqueness. The first tagline has better performance than the second tagline, and this makes a good case for prioritising the first tagline.

If no clear winners for an asset type exist, but it is an asset type you want to invest in, then consult your creative agencies as they may see greater longevity or creative potential in one asset compared to other options. If, after that process, still nothing separates these assets, then just pick one to prioritise. Which asset is picked will be less important than declaring one as a priority, so resources can be focused on building that asset rather than being split amongst several assets of the same type.

Identify the priorities in each asset type, and then subject them each to the usability criteria test covered in the *investment potential* quadrant discussion. This should lead you to identify a couple of assets to prioritise for investment, to turn the lake into a mountain peak.

The crowded tabletop

A crowded-tabletop structure is characterised by many usable assets.

This often reflects big, first-mover brands, with large advertising budgets, that have introduced innovations into the category. With each innovation, new assets have been added to the pool, and the number of assets has accumulated over time. In this scenario, competitors are often weak or advertise little, so mental competition is, at least at this stage, low.

This is a nice place to start but having too many assets can cause problems in the long term. It can leave you with too many balls to juggle and the brand's assets can become vulnerable. Remember: assets need to be protected, and having many assets can leave too many frontiers to defend. New entrants can change the competitive position in a short period of time; reducing the number of assets to manage can therefore help prepare the brand for future competition.

To obtain a focused set of assets, go through the same prioritisation process as for the lake structure. Classify by asset type and look for clear winners for similar assets types, and, again, consult with agencies about creative potential to help identify priorities for the future. Your aim is a manageable, useful, diverse set of valuable Distinctive Assets.

What if my brand doesn't have any usable or investable assets?

First take some consolation in that your brand is not alone; other brands are in that same position. Indeed, all new launches start at this position. But if you feel you have tried to build Distinctive Assets and still none reach even investable status, think of this result as a reflection of an ineffective past and focus efforts to change the brand's trajectory and strengthen the brand's identity for the future.

While the bad news is your brand has no assets with a head start, the good news is your brand has clean slate to build a strong Distinctive Asset base for the future. A useful approach is to undertake these activities:

- map the current market to establish competitive no-go zones
- link in with media planning to select assets with maximum potential

- remember to consider both shopping and advertising asset opportunities.

Then start to build one or two useful assets.

The next section of the book explores different asset types, to help you when working with each asset type and to make smarter choices when selecting the assets to build. The first chapter in this section provides a framework of asset types and introduces the concept of a *Distinctive Asset palette*.

12

Types
of Distinctive Assets

JENNI ROMANIUK

While Distinctive Assets can be almost anything that hits the senses, most people only focus on the holy trinity of colour, logo and tagline. The next chapters are to encourage you to broaden your ideas for potential Distinctive Assets, to introduce the concept of the *Distinctive Asset palette*, and to explore in greater depth the strengths and weaknesses of specific asset types.

Distinctive Assets are a sensory experience

Any stimulus is first processed into our sensory memory as we see, hear, smell, taste or touch something (Tulving & Craik, 2000). While Distinctive Assets often affect sight and hearing, the other senses—smell, taste and touch—can be activated under the right conditions. For example the retail environments of Lush Cosmetics and Abercrombie & Fitch have specific in-store scents, while the W hotel chain even sells its scent to take home (unfortunately it does not come with room service!).

Assets that activate smell, taste and touch add neurological diversity to the branding options; unfortunately, these asset types lack flexibility and adaptability. These assets only work if the buyer is in an environment you can influence or is willing to do some work to achieve asset exposure.

Scent-based assets are only useful if the buyer is physically present in the same environment or the buyer takes the scent home with them. And while some brands have a unique taste, this is only activated post-purchase. This makes leveraging taste Distinctive Assets for brand growth difficult, as brand growth requires reaching out to non-users or light users who have not tasted the brand, or did so a long time ago (Sharp, 2010a).

The product or packaging can activate our sense of touch. Remember: part of the original brief for the Coca-Cola bottle was to design something that could be identified by touch alone in the dark (Ryan, 2015). Unless, like the Coca-Cola bottle, this shape can also translate to be noticed in a two-dimensional environment, this type of asset also only works where the product is tangible, noticed and in the same physical environment as the category buyer. While there are some situations where activating these senses can be useful, these situations are often few.

Hearing and vision are the two senses often targeted by Distinctive Assets, as these senses can be activated in buying situations and during media consumption. These two senses offer a rich field of Distinctive Asset choices, and therefore the remainder of this chapter, and the next five chapters, focus on assets that draw on these senses.

Types of visual and audio assets

There is a big world of Distinctive Assets, so it is useful to have a schema of asset types to help navigate the options. Figure 12.1 shows visual assets classed into five broad types: colours, words, human faces, shapes and story; and audio assets into two broad types: sound and music.

Each asset type has sub-options. For example colour assets can be a single colour, a colour combination or a colour-based pattern; face assets can be a spokesperson, a character or a celebrity; and music can be a background instrumental piece, a jingle or a popular song.

These asset types can provide a large pool of options to inspire Distinctive Assets choices. The next five chapters cover how each

Figure 12.1: A schema of visual and audio Distinctive Asset types

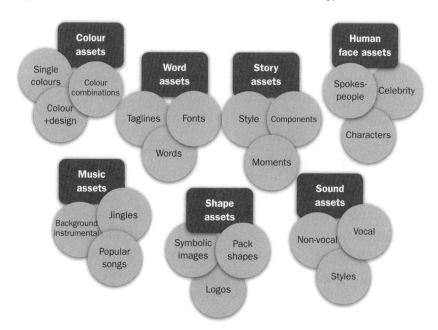

contributes to branding, with examples and the current evidence on effectiveness. But, before the detail in each individual chapter, it is useful to have an overall long-term goal for the brand's asset-building activities. This is referred to as a *Distinctive Asset palette*.

Creating a Distinctive Asset palette

Similar to a painter's palette, a Distinctive Asset palette is the menu of assets that provides options for branding in any environment. Like any menu, variety increases the chance that you will find the best option for any specific situation. Understanding the different asset types, and the benefits and drawbacks each provides, will help to identify which assets are better choices to add or develop.

The analogy with a menu is deliberate, as a common mistake when a brand has several Distinctive Assets is to treat these assets as an ingredient list, and mandate all assets have to always be included in every touch-point.

Not only is this unnecessary to achieve branding goals, it can create too many constraints and therefore stifle creative quality.

How many assets should a brand have?

Relying on only one asset is risky, as there may be challenges to this or situations where it is not an effective choice. Having a wide number of assets is also risky, as too many options to manage fragments resources, and leaves assets open to decay and competitor attack. Drawing on the goals of Distinctive Assets that provide flexibility, adaptability and neurological diversity, around four or five assets are enough to achieve these goals, without leaving the brand vulnerable.

While a good palette will have a set of about four or five assets, the viable list of assets will depend on the brand's circumstances. Here are two factors to consider in determining the number and types of assets:

- *media and distribution channel diversity*—the wider the range of channels where you promote or sell your brand, the greater the number of assets your brand might need to achieve optimal branding in each environment. Your brand doesn't need a separate asset for each medium or shopping format, but examine what will work best in each of the options where the brand has a decent amount of resources allocated, and design the brand's Distinctive Asset palette accordingly.
- *above-the-line (ATL) advertising spend level*—ATL spend helps to build assets amongst the people you need to reach and teach—non-users and new category buyers. The lower the brand's spend, the longer it will take to build assets, so aim for fewer but more valuable assets. But if the brand advertises extensively and continually, such as supermarkets or department store retailers, which are often on air every week with new messages, then a larger menu of Distinctive Assets can stop creative and consumer wear-out due to frequent use of the same assets.

While Figure 12.2 illustrates a brand with a Distinctive Asset palette of one of every major type of asset, this comprehensiveness is a longer-term goal. In the short term, what is important is that the brand has at least one asset as close to 100% Fame and 100% Uniqueness as possible and that, when assets are added, this is thoughtfully done, with variety in mind.

Figure 12.2: Distinctive Asset palette framework

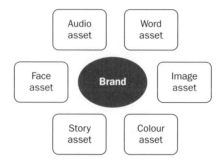

Should the likeability of the asset matter?

Often, when deciding among a wide array of assets, it can seem sensible to consult consumers, ask category buyers to rate their liking of different assets, and select the most liked asset. While potential assets that stimulate disgust might be obvious candidates for avoidance[1], an asset should not be disregarded just because it is not liked immediately.

Familiarity and liking have a relationship such that, as someone is more often exposed to a stimulus, a subconscious mechanism makes that person like that stimulus more (Zajonc, 1968). The more often the brand uses an asset, the more the liking of that asset will grow.

The brand doesn't therefore need an asset to start with a highly positive attitude amongst category buyers, as this immediate subjective assessment is likely to be fickle, with asset liking coinciding with effective execution. Usefulness, diversity and current performance on metrics are more sensible criteria for asset selection as these are linked to the asset's ability to do its job for the brand. There is more on this in the next chapter on colour assets.

The following chapters explore the different asset types in greater detail. The first of these chapters investigates colour assets, why these are useful to build and why, as detailed in Chapters 5 and 10, colour assets tend to underperform other assets.

---

1   It does depend on the objective, as I suspect aesthetics were not high on the list when John Oliver offered 'Jeff the Diseased Lung' to tobacco companies as a spokesmodel (Lopez, 2015).

13

Building Colour-based Distinctive Assets

Everything visual has a colour. But, while decisions about colour are unavoidable, you do need to make an active decision to cultivate a colour-based Distinctive Asset, as these don't evolve on their own. Colour-based assets include the following:

- a single colour (red)
- a colour combination (red and yellow)
- a colour-and-design combination (a red circle).

This chapter highlights the benefits, challenges and common pitfalls that face those who prioritise colour assets. It builds on Chapter 5, which showed the mismatch between the desire for a colour-based asset and the branding performance of this type of asset.

Why colour-based assets are useful

Colour is a big part of our lives. Colours stimulate our emotions: red is exciting and blue is calming. Tone of colour also matters: a bright colour signals freshness and vibrancy; a dull colour, the opposite. Then there are the meanings that underpin different colours (semiotics)—white signalling purity; black, sophistication and so on. While interesting, these ideas can distract from making smart choices about colour in a brand's identity, because they miss the role and value of colour as a Distinctive Asset.

ORANGE—WHICH CAME FIRST: THE FRUIT OR THE COLOUR?

The fruit, which was named from the Sanskrit *naranga* in the 1300s, became *orenge* in Old French and then was converted to *orange* in English. When the fruit became widely available in English markets, in the 1600s, the word *orange* replaced the previous word for the colour, *geoluread*, which is red-yellow in Old English. So the fruit came first.

This is also why a robin redbreast is so named, even though the colour of the breast is orange. The bird was named before the colour orange existed (Soniak, 2012).

First, let's consider why your brand might want to build a colour-based asset.

Look around quickly and what do you see? Most likely you see a blurry, colourful, world. This is because colour is the only thing our eyes can take in when we scan a scene without fixing on any specific object (Wedel & Pieters, 2006). Only after fixing your visual field can you process shape, words and other visual features. This makes a colour Distinctive Asset a powerful way to find a brand in a cluttered environment, whether that be the blur of green that signals Starbucks and simplifies the search for coffee, the bright pink that signals Vanish in a supermarket as you scan the shelves, or the flash of yellow that tells you the advertisement is for Pedigree dog food.

Prior chapters highlighted the power of colour as a way for consumers to find brands (Gaillard, Sharp & Romaniuk, 2006; Piñero et al., 2010), and also the systematically lower Uniqueness of colour assets compared to other assets (Ward, 2017). But before delving into the challenges of building colour assets, let's first examine the different types of colour assets.

Types of colour assets

This section explores the three broad types of colour assets: single-colour assets, colour combinations and colour-and-design combinations.

Single-colour assets

Single-colour assets form when an individual colour is linked to the brand. Well-known examples include purple for Cadbury chocolate, red for Vodafone, or yellow for Pedigree dog food. As illustrated in Chapter 5 with packaging assets, individual colours are some of the most common assets suggested for testing, and one of the areas where marketers are often disappointed with results.

Before a colour can be a contender for a brand's Distinctive Asset, it needs to pass through three filters (Figure 13.1). A colour can signal a category (such as red signalling the ketchup section), a subcategory (such as white signalling the cream pasta sauces, or red signalling chilli is present in the product) or a brand (such as purple signalling Cadbury). Once you have discounted the colours that signal the category, subcategories and competitors, the remaining colours are options for the brand to adopt.

Figure 13.1: The colour-screening questions

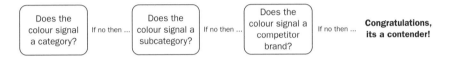

Colour combinations

The list of potential colours that remain after the three screening questions can often be short and uninspiring. If this happens, an alternative is to build links to a colour combination. Examples include Pepsi's red and blue, Mars chocolate's red and black or the colours that appear in the Google logo (can you name them?[1]). The testing of colour combinations reveals no difference in the performance of colour combination assets when compared to single-colour assets (Ward, 2017). Colour combinations are not therefore easier or more difficult to own as Distinctive Assets compared to single colours.

To build a colour combination as a Distinctive Asset, the colours that make up the combination need to be used simultaneously (for example red

---

1   Blue, red, yellow and green.

and white together). Ranges of colours used across the brand's products (one pack in pale pink, another in pale blue, another in pale green) typically score poorly. For example when we tested a colour range for a brand in a household care category in the USA, it scored 3% Fame and 29% Uniqueness. These low scores are indicative of the scores achieved in other testing of similar types of colour-range assets. It is more difficult to build a colour range because category buyers rarely experience enough of the range with sufficient frequency to make the overall connection between all the colours and the brand name.

The reverse is also the case. It is dangerous to assume that because your brand has a strong colour combination, each of the single colours will work just as well individually. It may be only one colour of the combination has sufficient strength as an individual Distinctive Asset to be used in isolation. Gathering appropriate metrics, before making any decision to use an individual colour from a colour combination, can help avoid costly mistakes.

Colour-and-design combinations

The third way to build a colour-based asset is to bundle colour with a design element, such as a shape, to create a Distinctive Asset. Examples include HSBC's use of red borders around its advertising and Red Bull's can with the slanted blue and silver rectangles. This combination of design and colour can create greater Uniqueness than a solo colour, and become a valuable Distinctive Asset. The limitation is that the introduction of a design element puts some constraints on the colour's use, as it always has to be in combination with the design to build and utilise the Distinctive Asset. As with deconstructing a colour combination, find appropriate metrics for the individual components before decoupling the colour and design components and using either separately. A valuable asset in combination does not guarantee each of the individual parts is equally valuable.

If going down this route, be wary of incorporating colours that are strong Distinctive Assets for competitors' brands. The strength of a colour-and-design asset takes time to build and, in the interim, you risk benefiting a competitor's brand if category buyers think of the competitor when they see the asset.

Why colour-based assets are challenging to build

While there is considerable evidence that highlights the importance of colour to our visual systems when findings brands, colour-based assets prove difficult to build. Two key challenges that marketers face when building a Distinctive Asset are the tendency of colour to blend into the background, and for marketers to get bored or look for easy routes to change.

Colour versus the environment

Colour is everywhere and, for a specific colour to be noticed, it has to dominate the scene. Without executional prominence, our brain pays attention to something else, such as a cute puppy. While all assets fight for attention, colour is so integral to multifaceted scenes of shapes, faces and other neurologically rich items that it often slips under the radar.

While colour is a part of a pack, logo or font, these items are more likely to be processed holistically, rather than as a separate colour–brand link. This is evident in the poor scores typically achieved when testing colour as a separate asset: for example the colour the brand name is written in as a potential colour asset (separate from the text usage). Despite the constant presence of a colour in the brand name, it is only registers as a potential Distinctive Asset when the colour is also used outside the brand-name context.

Table 13.1 shows an example of results for testing the whole logo for a brand versus its component parts of images, colour and font. The logo has investment potential in the first country and is in the use-or-lose quadrant in the second country. Even though all of the elements are in the logo, only the character, which also appears in advertising, performs at a similar level to the whole logo. The colour of the font did not score at all in either

Table 13.1: Whole logo asset strength versus its parts—first example

	Country 1		Country 2	
	Fame (%)	Uniqueness (%)	Fame (%)	Uniqueness (%)
Character in logo	32	96	83	100
Font in logo	4	79	68	97
Image in logo	3	8	8	16
Font colour	0	0	0	0
Whole logo	36	96	83	100

country, while the font is only of value as an individual asset in one of the two countries.

In another example of a more conventional logo, without an eye-catching character (Table 13.2), the whole logo is an investable asset, as is the font. But the background colour and the font colour are both in the ignore-or-test quadrant.

Table 13.2: Whole logo asset strength versus its parts—second example

	Fame (%)	Uniqueness (%)
Image in logo	26	90
Font in logo	23	94
Logo background colour	13	48
Font colour	1	9
Whole logo	**29**	**96**

To build colour as a specific Distinctive Asset, the execution needs to involve colour being called out as an entity that is separate from the other parts of the scene or logo. This allows the colour to form its own separate association with the brand name and to act as a cue to trigger the brand.

Colour versus the easily bored

Colour is a decision that is continually remade when each new piece of visual branded material is released to the world. This makes colour prone to variation simply for the sake of variety. In a survey of brand managers and agency staff by Newstead (2014), managers were asked which they considered to be more acceptable to change in a logo: the colour, shape or typeface. Colour was the feature most often acceptable for change, particularly when managers were pressured to reinvigorate the brand. It is also one of the easiest features to change, which makes it an attractive option to 'freshen up' a brand.

Should consumer preferences matter when selecting colour assets?

'What's your favourite colour?' is a question that young children use to bond. Most of us have colours we prefer, and others we like less. Indeed a research team in Australia claim to have found the ugliest colour in world—Pantone 448-C—to put on cigarette packs to discourage smoking (Lang, 2016).

My favourite colour is purple. I have purple clothes, my bedroom wall is painted purple and, when choosing the colour for the splashback in my kitchen, guess what colour I chose? So when choosing a colour for the cover of this book—did I want it to be purple? Absolutely. But how much should my liking of purple, or anyone else's liking of purple, affect that cover choice?

Let's first unpack why people's liking a colour is thought to matter. The basic premise involves two ideas that are commonplace in psychological theories on branding: attention and attitude transfer.

First, the attention model is that if you like a colour you are, perhaps, likely to notice things in that colour—so the presence of that colour will attract your attention. Second, the attitude model is that if you like a colour, you then might transfer this liking of the colour to a brand with that colour. Both of these mechanisms could lead you to buy brands in that colour.

Imagine if this did work: what would my world look like? Well, first I would have a home awash with purple products everywhere—not just in my wardrobe, but in my kitchen and bathroom. I'd brush my teeth with Crest 3D White, wash my clothes with Purex and Crystals Fragrance Fresh Lavender Blossom, and dine on Annie's Rotini Pasta with a three-cheese sauce. Given few brands are purple, I would also be loyal to these brands (particularly Annie's Rotini Pasta as, after looking through over 200 pasta sauce options on walmart.com this was the only purple option I could find). But a quick look in my cupboards would reveal a rainbow of colours, with little purple in sight.

Now, I accept that using myself as an example is hardly a rigorous test of the role of colour preferences in Distinctive Assets, so let's look at some more robust empirical evidence. Perhaps the attentional advantage of using a colour that category buyers like makes it easier for each person to develop the link between the colour and the brand. This could create an advantage for a more popular colour over a less popular colour, when building a Distinctive Asset.

If liking a colour helps build Distinctive Assets, there should be a relationship between how much a colour is liked and the level of colour–brand linkage. The testing of this hypothesis is over three categories: chocolate, banking and haircare (127 colour-brand combinations in total)[2].

Category buyers ranked the colours in the survey from most to least liked. The top three–ranked colours were dark blue, light blue and red, while brown, orange and pink comprised the bottom three rankings. The results show the correlations between brand–colour linkage scores and colour ranking are low (0.36 for banking, –0.28 for chocolate and –0.12 for haircare). This says that more liked colours were not stronger Distinctive Assets. Figure 13.2 shows a scatter plot of the results for each category.

Figure 13.2: The relationship between colour-liking rank and Distinctive Asset strength

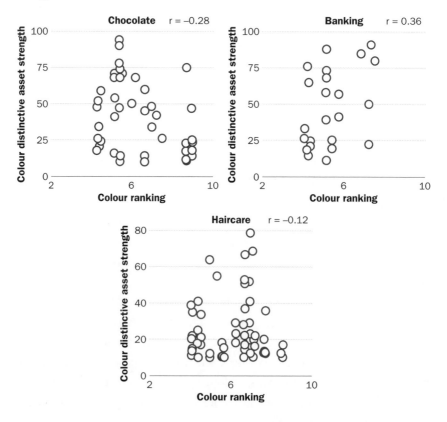

---

2   These results are from an online survey of 880 Australian consumers conducted in October 2009.

The next stage tested, at individual level, whether respondents who linked a brand to a colour tended to have greater liking for that colour than those who did not form those same brand linkages. In 94% of the individual brand–asset tests, there was no relationship between individuals' liking of the colour and their linking of a brand to that colour. Liking of a colour does not affect the creation of a colour as a valuable Distinctive Asset.

Figure 13.3 shows the results by category.

Figure 13.3: Brand–colour linkage and liking the colour

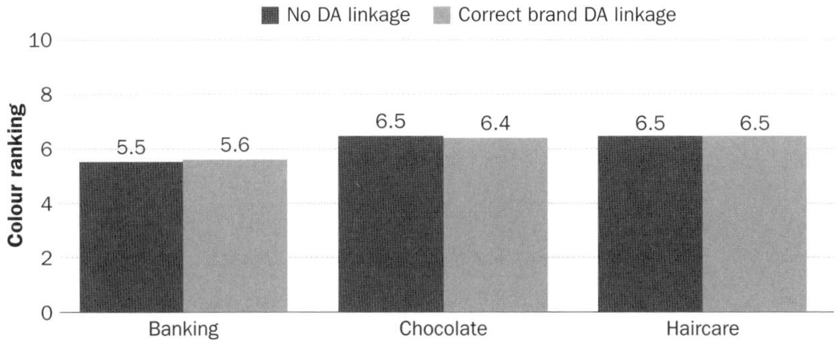

Protecting colour assets

When it comes to colour, there is a clearly apparent disconnect between desire and practice. Colour is a desirable asset for a brand to own, but the evidence suggests marketers are doing a poor job in developing colours as Distinctive Assets. If you do have a brand with a colour asset, protect it at all costs as there will come a time when other people in the company or your agencies start telling you they (or consumers) are tired of it and they think the brand's colour needs to change.

If that happens, congratulate yourself. But don't change the colour. It's one of the most valuable assets your brand can develop—so protect it. Chapter 18 covers how to handle requests or pressure to freshen or update a brand's identity.

Next we will cover shapes and story assets; these include logos, advertising moments and styles.

14

Assets that Draw on Shapes and Build Stories

JENNI ROMANIUK

This chapter covers two types of assets: shapes, which are visual assets including logos, symbolic images such as product forms, and pack shapes; and story assets. These assets integrate into advertising's creative design and can range from an overall advertising style to a more specific moment or component such as an animal.

Types of shape assets

As a category, shape Distinctive Assets cover elements that have a visual form in two or three dimensions. Shapes can tap into the rich visual processing system we use to recognise shapes and the familiar. This type of asset is also helpful to provide contrast in text-rich environments, such as in storied print media (Smit, Boerman & Van Meurs, 2015). This chapter will cover three common types of shape assets: the logo, symbols and pack shapes.

Logo shapes

Shapes are often used in the construction of logos, forming part or all of a logo. These shapes can be common, such as a circle for Pepsi, or unusual such as Krispy Kreme's pentagonal shape. A common shape can be a Distinctive Asset, if it is uncommon in the category and has other qualities to help build its Uniqueness. For example with Pepsi, the common circular shape is combined with the blue-and-red swirl inside. Logo shapes can also be visual representations of the brand name, such as the T for T-mobile or the two red bulls for, you guessed it, Red Bull.

While the presence of logo shapes might be ubiquitous, the link between the shape in isolation and the brand name can be tenuous if the shape has always been executed as a background component. Without prominent use, people tend to process the logo as a whole, and not form separate links to a specific shape (as discussed for colour in Chapter 13).

Logo shapes have considerable adaptability as Distinctive Assets, as they can be used in a variety of visual platforms, as well as across in-store and online shopping environments. For example Amazon's smile appears on a billboard in Time Square, on boxes that deliver goods purchased on Amazon, on the website, on the clothing of staff, in television advertising, on the front of the retail store in Manhattan, on bags used to pack purchases from the store, and on the thumbnail image accompanying its many apps. Everywhere visual that Amazon is, its smile can appear.

One of the newer roles for logo shapes is as thumbnail images for apps. Some thumbnails contain the brand name, others images from the logo. For example Airbnb just has an image of its logo, while Expedia includes the brand name. Given most phones and tablets are cluttered with many different apps, having a strong logo as a Distinctive Asset can help users to find an app. But consistency in asset usage is important.

For example I have two news apps on my phone. One is the BBC app, which has the letters BBC on three white squares, consistent with its website and television logos. The second is the Huffington Post app, which was a green H, but is now a broken green square on a black background that I still have trouble finding because my brain became trained to look for the H. Apparently this is an abstract H (Beizer & Zack, 2017), but my brain doesn't register it as such and it still takes me much longer to find it on my phone. If the brand's activities have trained category buyers to find a specific symbol, try to avoid change, as you then may lose out to a competitor's app.

Symbols

The most cited epitome of symbolic shape Distinctive Assets is the Nike 'swoosh'. But most people forget that there was not some magic awakening of the collective conscious that linked that image to Nike in our brains. This link got there through decades of prominent co-presentation in advertising and on pack. Yes it is strong now, but it was not always. Nor will it always be unless Nike keeps refreshing those memory structures in existing category buyers, as well as building these links amongst new category buyers.

Similar to colours, there is a rich field of research into the semiotics of shapes, and what curves or sharp angles might implicitly convey. But the priority for Distinctive Asset usage is whether a shape could be owned by the brand, which, if that happens, should supersede the role of any other meaning.

One of the most common symbols we test is the product form. This can be in food products, such as a bar of chocolate or a shape of a cracker; it can also be in household products, such as dishwasher tablets or laundry capsules. In services it can be tangible items that represent the product, such as credit cards or ATMs, while in durables it can be the shape of the car, a computer, a mobile phone or part of these products such as the badge or headphone shape. Examples of well-known product forms include Viagra's pill, the Mini Cooper car, and the classic iMac.

Product forms suffer from two major disadvantages that mean these rarely become strong assets. First, unless externally visible, most of the reinforcement is only with users after they have bought the product. Indeed when we compare the results for brand users with non-users (as discussed in Chapter 9), typically product-form assets have a much greater gap in scores than other assets.

Second, many product forms within the same category look similar, with differences so subtle that they are only identifiable by an expert with a wide range of product forms visible side by side. This means product forms from different brands are confused, creating uncertainty and a lack of Uniqueness.

For product forms to become Distinctive Assets, they first have to look different from other product forms and, second, the product form needs to be visible to brand non-users. This visibility to non-users can be via advertising, or visual presence on pack. A good example of this is Apple's integration of the white headphones in its advertising. Indeed the success in the initial stages led to claims that thieves were targeting people wearing white headphones as this signalled to them that the person had an Apple product and so was a valuable mugging target (Coté, 2007).

Pack shapes

As covered in Chapter 5, while packaging protects a product, it can have a secondary role as a Distinctive Asset. This can include the total pack such as the triangle shape of Toblerone, or some particular part of it, such as the neck in Duck toilet cleaner. That packs need to be packed, stored and transported puts a limit on the range of packaging options. Further, given today's e-commerce and m-commerce world, an important quality of pack shapes, similar to apps, is the ability retain distinctiveness when small and seen in two dimensions.

Therefore, when designing or deciding on pack shape as an asset, check if the shape is or could be identifiable in all current and potential shopping environments. If this is not possible, that doesn't mean a packaging Distinctive Asset can't be developed, as illustrated by San Pellegrino, where the addition of a foil covering turns an ordinary can shape into a potential Distinctive Asset.

Distinctive Assets that tell stories

Story assets are Distinctive Assets that become integrated into the creative design, and often form the basis for storylines. The focus here is on three types of story assets:

- *styles*—which permeate the entire advertisement, such as the cartoon style of Red Bull

- *moments*—specific actions or visuals that occur at a specific point in time, such as the nose tap used by Rajah spices in South Africa
- *components*—specific items that can be incorporated into creative design, such as the Andrex puppy or the Aflac duck.

Story assets can separate from the creative design and become Distinctive Assets when these assets reappear over multiple executions. This reappearance gives the asset the potential to become an association with the brand that is separate from any specific advertisement. The first challenge when building this type of asset is to pinpoint the exact association that will become linked to the brand name. Is the specific asset how it looks (a style), what happens (a moment) or something contained in the moment (a component)? Specifying the asset allows everyone involved with the brand's marketing activities to understand what needs to be kept consistent to keep building and strengthening the asset, but also frees up creativity by identifying factors available for change.

Styles

A style is something that flows through the entire advertisement. Examples of styles include animation, such as used by Red Bull; the type of location, such as the white laboratory style of Progressive; or linguistic styles, such as Mastercard's 'priceless' campaigns. An advertising style is often executed early, which allows this type of Distinctive Asset to provide early branding signals without directly mentioning the brand name (and overcomes one of the major barriers in brand execution discussed in Chapter 4).

But advertising styles can feel limiting, with marketers and creative staff getting bored with even the most effective campaigns. This is evident in how even styles that are lauded are either used intermittently or dropped in favour of something new. For example in a review of sixty-one different executions from Progressive Insurance over the last few years, the white laboratory style only featured at the start of the advertisement in one-third of cases. The remaining two-thirds either did not feature the setting or, in the case of five executions, the white lab was featured later on in the advertisement. In a similar vein, Geico continues to have multiple styles that depart from its best-known advertising style that features the wisecracking, English-accented gecko. Unless all advertising styles are of equal strength, or the direct branding is enhanced to compensate for the weaker style, it is likely these brands pay a branding penalty for deviating from the best-known styles.

One example of advertising style longevity is Mastercard's 'priceless' campaign, started in 1997. Absolut Vodka's style that involves the bottle shape is another such long-standing campaign, which debuted in 1980 with a single execution that included the bottle, a halo and the words 'Absolut perfection' (Taube, 2013). But these cases, in their long lifespans, are notable as exceptions.

If employing an advertising style as a Distinctive Asset, it is therefore useful to consider early potential challenges to its longevity and how these might be avoided when settling on the elements of the style that will remain consistent in the long term. The final choice needs to achieve easy-to-process similarity without constraining creative ideas.

Moments

Moments offer greater flexibility than styles, as these only take up part of an advertisement. But the challenge is to specify the 'event' that is going to be repeated and become linked to the brand, as moments are often made up of multiple elements. Knowing what to keep and what to change in a moment is key to building this type of Distinctive Asset. This requires considering component and execution factors.

In terms of components, moments that use the product, such as pouring milk onto cereal or opening a can of drink, risk looking generic, which makes it difficult to develop a specific association between that common moment and your brand. To make a product-based moment a Distinctive Asset, think of some unique twist on the product use. Some useful examples are Oreo's Twist, Lick, Dunk, the Tim Tam Slam, or when someone in a Skittles advertisement touches something and it turns to Skittles.

Similar to a colour range, it is more difficult to be known for something as broad as 'having children' or 'having dogs', than to be linked to a specific child or animal type. Moments involving an action can be easier to own, as the actions have the potential to be performed in multiple contexts and by multiple people, which increases the flexibility.

Components

Components are specific items that can be incorporated in different circumstances. For example a specific breed of dog such as the West Highland white terrier in the My Dog advertising, the Old English sheepdog in the Dulux advertisements, or the white headphones in an iPod advertisement. These components are often integrated into the storyline without being the focal point, which makes it important that the groundwork to build up the link with the brand name is completed first, if these are to become Distinctive Assets.

Relying on implicit association over time is a risky strategy. For components, it is also important to identify the memory structure you are building: is it the presence of a dog or the presence of that type of dog? Once specified, don't deviate too much from this central idea, at least in the first few years of using that asset. Too much variation too quickly is not friendly to building category buyers' mental structures.

The next chapter covers another type of asset—faces of the brand, which includes celebrities, characters and spokespeople.

15

Faces of a Brand—Celebrities, Spokespeople and Characters

JENNI ROMANIUK

One of our evolutionary instincts is to notice faces, first and foremost, in any scene (Gobbini et al., 2013). We are hard-wired to notice faces, and so something with a face attracts our attention. As previously mentioned, our brain even has the fusiform face area, which is a specific location that lights up neurologically when we see any human face (Kanwisher, McDermott & Chun, 1997). This expertise in reading faces harks back to our sociological survival skills. When someone approaches, looking at their facial expression is one way to quickly determine if that person is a friend or a foe, and whether you should therefore approach or run in the other direction.

Faces can also talk and express emotion, which creates rich signals for the brain to process. The personality of the face of a brand can set the tone of the brand's communication and influence creative strategy. The key interest in this chapter is on faces as branding devices: when and how a brand can use a face to trigger a brand name. Celebrities, while getting a great deal of attention, are just one type of face for a brand; spokespeople (for example Flo from Progressive) and characters (such as Red and Yellow from M&M's) are also ways of giving the brand a face. This chapter covers these three types of faces for a brand.

The lure of celebrity

It is a truth universally acknowledged that a brand, in possession of good equity, must be in want of a celebrity[1]. Current estimates are that, around the world, one in five advertisements contain a celebrity (Knoll & Matthes, 2017). In some categories, such as skin care and athletic shoes, and in countries such as China, Japan or South Korea, celebrity endorsement is the advertising strategy *du jour*.

What makes someone a celebrity? In today's fifteen-seconds-of-fame society it can be challenging to answer this question. In the academic literature, someone becomes a celebrity endorser when they are familiar to an audience, and they use this recognition to promote a brand (McCracken, 1989). The extent of that celebrity depends on how many people know who they are—the greater recognition, the greater the level of celebrity. Previously, celebrities came from the confines of a couple of key entertainment areas such as movies, music, television or sports. Today's celebrities are sourced from widespread areas such as cooking, gardening, reality television or online channels such as YouTube, where, for example, PewDiePie has more than fifty million subscribers (McAlone, 2017), which makes him better known than most television actors.

The familiarity effect that comes from recognising a celebrity differs from the influence effect of taking cues on how to think or behave from them. This difference is often confused. For example I can recognise Kate Moss, but not care about her opinion sufficiently to act on her endorsement of a make-up brand. Previously, the influence part of celebrity, the ability to move the masses, came from expertise in a specific area (Bergkvist & Zhou, 2016). For example athletes would previously endorse athletic products, such as the basketball player LeBron James with

---

1   With apologies to Jane Austen.

athletic shoes. The influence came from the area of a celebrity's expertise and their capacity to know which is the best for that area. If LeBron James uses Nike, this brand of shoe must be the best because he is an excellent basketball player and he could buy any shoes in the world.

Today, celebrities are stretched to endorse brands in categories significantly beyond those linked to their expertise. For example LeBron James has endorsed Sprite, Kia, Wheaties and McDonald's. These brands are leveraging LeBron James's fame as a well-known face, rather than his automotive or nutrition expertise. The social media world is even more complicated as celebrities are also paid for their audience, which are the followers they have on Instagram, Twitter or Facebook, and this can be substantial. In June 2017 Katy Perry became the first person to reach 100 million followers on Twitter (Fisher, 2017).

Faces naturally attract attention, and celebrities can be considered as expensive faces, with costs up to $50 million for the likes of Beyoncé and George Clooney (AJ, 2015). The additional expense (over a cheaper, non-celebrity person) is in the hope is that the increased cost of a celebrity presence will be offset by the impression, whether through advertising or social media, having a greater impact. But the qualities that attract marketers to invest in a celebrity might also hamper the effectiveness of celebrities as branding devices.

Celebrity face versus normal face

While faces quickly attract attention, familiar faces attract attention with even greater speed. In a crowded room, you quickly notice your friends over strangers. The knowledge you have about a celebrity creates a similar sense of familiarity, which gives the celebrity face an attentional advantage, compared to other faces. This feeling of familiarity comes from the size of *their* associative network in *your* memory.

To illustrate this, think about a good friend, someone you know well. What thoughts come to mind? Go through the thoughts you associate with that friend. These thoughts are part of the associative network that you have in your memory for that friend—a rich network of interlinked thoughts. Remember back to the idea of cued retrieval from Chapter 2— when you think of or see that friend, these are thoughts that can be retrieved. When you see something related to these thoughts, you can also think of your friend. An advertisement for a movie reminds you of the time you both saw it at the cinema, walking past a Thai restaurant reminds you of that trip to Thailand you both took: your friend can pop into your mind because of your memories formed from past experiences.

Now think of a celebrity, say Jennifer Lopez, and conduct a similar exercise. Think of all the things you know about Jennifer Lopez. On that list you might have thoughts about her music, movies, television shows, her performing in Las Vegas, past husbands, her children, her outfit at the Grammies and so on.

Now look at the young woman in Figure 15.1. What thoughts come to mind when you see her? Given you probably don't know her, chances are it is a short list of thoughts. This is a similar reaction to what you might have when you see an unknown person in an advertisement. When you see

Figure 15.1: A young woman[2]

2   This is my niece, Madelene, someone I have a very rich network of associations about!

someone you don't know, all you have is what is in front of you to stimulate thoughts; no past memories to access.

In terms of your memory structures, a known celebrity resembles a friend more than a stranger—with a node and a set of (often extensive) linked associations in your memory. This memory network gives the gifts of attention and image transfer. Without this network, a celebrity is just another face in an advertisement—useful, yes, but not worth the additional expense over any other face. But this network that makes a celebrity feel familiar comes with drawbacks as well as benefits, when using the celebrity as a branding device to trigger the brand name.

A celebrity as a branding device

When Allstate Insurance uses Dennis Haysbert at the start of an advertisement, he can be a branding device to trigger Allstate, if Allstate is absent at that time. This can only happen if the link between Dennis Haysbert and Allstate has been established. Chapter 2 covered the role of mental competition and how its presence makes it difficult to attach a brand to an asset. A large associative network already attached to the celebrity means it will be more difficult for the brand to become a salient part of the celebrity's network in someone's memory (Meyers-Levy, 1989). For example if I know a great deal about Jennifer Lopez or George Clooney, then any brand she or he endorses has to wiggle its way into my already extensive network if the brand is going to have any chance of being retrieved when I see these celebrities.

A successful brand attachment is just the first part of the challenge of using a celebrity as a branding device. The second part is to keep the brand as a fresh part of the network, fresher than memories for movies, television shows, gossip about private life and so on. Unlike other assets with meaning, celebrities usually engage in activities to keep themselves topical, such as promoting their own activities or posting items about their life on social media. This freshens the brand's mental competition. When I see Katy Perry, do I think of CoverGirl, or do I think of her new album, her feud with Taylor Swift or how she publicly ranked three of her lovers? In essence, the entire publicity machine of the celebrity indirectly works against the memory for the brands the celebrity endorses. This means the more famous the celebrity, and the more often they are in the press for non-brand activities, the greater the difficulty for that celebrity to become a strong Distinctive Asset for a brand.

Mental competition with celebrity endorsers

Celebrities, with their non–brand name associative networks, and the brand, mentally compete in two key ways (see Figure 15.2): within the creative environment (competition for attention) and in competition for brand retrieval.

Figure 15.2: Two types of celebrity mental competition

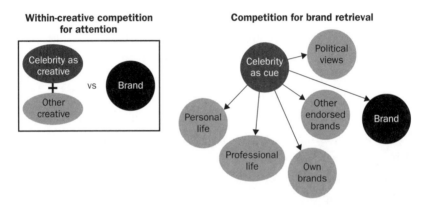

1 *Within the creative environment (competition for attention)*: Within the creative environment (advertisement, Instagram picture, Facebook video), the celebrity can distract the viewer away from the brand. Popularly referred to as the 'vampire effect', work by Erfgen, Zenker and Sattler (2015) shows the vampire effect in print advertising, where celebrity-based advertising suffered lower recall than the same advertisements with equally attractive non-celebrity substitutes. Our attention to advertising is limited, and the known celebrity takes up extra attention, which leaves less time to attend to the brand name. In Erfgen and colleagues (2015), celebrities only had a positive effect on brand recall when the link between the brand and the celebrity was strong. This suggests the vampire effect might be caused by weak celebrity ties to the brand—the stronger the link, the greater the probability that when the celebrity is noticed, the brand will also

be noticed or evoked. We see this in our own research, where the link between the brand and the celebrity is 4.5 times stronger when category buyers know the celebrity's name (Romaniuk, Nguyen & Simmonds, 2017).

2 *Competition for brand retrieval*: a benefit of a celebrity endorser is that they have a life outside the advertisement, and so can act as a cue for the brand in a wide range of contexts. For example I am at home watching Wimbledon; if Roger Federer is playing, seeing him could trigger Credit Suisse. In this case Credit Suisse competes with all the other associations I have for Roger Federer including his charity work with Rafael Nadal, that he has twins, and that he was given a cow for appearing in the Swiss Open. Sorry Credit Suisse, you have to be very strong to compete against twins and a cow!

It is easy to underestimate how widespread celebrity associative networks are, and thereby underestimate the amount of mental competition a brand faces. Recently, we surveyed around 600 people in the USA and asked them which brands they linked to twenty celebrities from movies, television, music and sports, including Taylor Swift, Serena Williams, Kevin Hart, Jennifer Garner and Selena Gomez.

Figure 15.3 details the four categories of brands we found attached to celebrities, and the average percentage attached to each type. The first

Figure 15.3: Types of brands linked to celebrities (average across twenty celebrities)

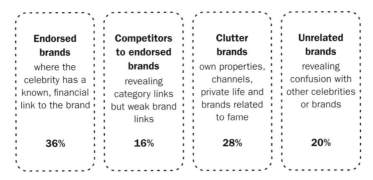

Online survey of 600 US adults conducted in July 2016

category is *endorsed brands*, which are brands with a declared financial relationship with the celebrity. The second category contains *competitor brands*, which are brands that compete in the same category as endorsed brands.

Clutter brands make up the third category; these are brands that are either the celebrities' own properties, such as the movie *Think Like a Man* for Kevin Hart; brands linked to celebrity fame, such as Wimbledon for Serena Williams; or brands linked to a celebrity's private life, such as Ben Affleck for Jennifer Garner. The fourth category was named *unrelated brands*, as it contained all the remaining brands that did not fit into the first three categories, and generally reflects confusion in brand and celebrity attribution.

The results show that endorsed brands are around one-third of the brands recalled, and that the second-largest category is clutter brands, which provide a greater level of mental competition for an endorsed brand than direct competitors. There were differences between celebrities, ranging from 71% of endorsed brand responses for Dennis Haysbert to only 8% of endorsed brand responses for Steve Harvey, but there were no significant differences between types of celebrities.

Why multiple endorsements muddy the retrieval pot

Remember that endorsed brands, as a category, also include all endorsed brands—and that this ranges from celebrities well known for a single endorsement such as Dennis Haysbert, whose endorsed brand links were 100% Allstate (when shown his picture, some consumers referred to him as 'the Allstate guy'), to celebrities with multiple endorsements such as Sofia Vergara, who was linked to CoverGirl, Kmart, Head & Shoulders, Diet Pepsi, Rooms To Go and Ninja coffee-maker.

In an example from another part of the world, Virat Kohli, an Indian cricket player, endorsed eighteen brands at the same time (Express Web Desk, 2017). While these brands are not in the same category (examples of endorsements include Audi cars, Tissot watches, Colgate toothpaste and Vicks lozenges), they still compete for mental attention; buyers seeing Kohli in your advertisement might retrieve another of his endorsed brands. If I see Roger Federer and think of Mercedes-Benz, this makes it less likely I will evoke Credit Suisse, as my memory lacks a direct link between Credit Suisse and Mercedes Benz—other than via Roger Federer. And my mind is just as likely to travel down the Mercedes-Benz path and think about my friend Max who is obsessed with old Mercedes, other cars, driving experiences and so on, rather than venture back to the Roger Federer node in my memory.

This type of mental competition means not only is the brand competing with the celebrity's personal and professional life for attention, it also competes with other brands attached to that celebrity in memory.

Celebrities are also not without risk. What do Accenture, Anheuser-Busch, Speedo and Tag Heuer all have in common? They have felt the sting of a celebrity endorsement gone wrong due to scandal. Celebrities can't be controlled, and contract clauses can't stop scandals happening—they just make it easier for the brand to be extricated when they occur.

Having a 'face' attached to the brand has attentional value but that face does not need to be a celebrity. It can be a spokesperson or a character to achieve some of the attention benefits, but none of the mental competition drawbacks. If you are thinking of using a celebrity as a branding device, then one who is familiar but who does not generate a great number of fresh, salient thoughts in category buyers (that is, someone who was famous three years ago) might be the most prudent choice. This could give the benefits of a familiar face, without the drawbacks of mental competition. Such a celebrity might also come a bit cheaper than someone who is currently 'hot'.

Spokespeople

While much of advertising contains people, some brands have a pattern of using the same person across campaigns. This person can develop into a Distinctive Asset. These (largely) unknown people become famous for being synonymous with the brand: for example Flo from Progressive, or the brunette woman for Trivago. Sometimes these people are performers (actors or comedians) but their commercial persona becomes more famous than their own or their professional persona. That these people are often unknown outside the advertisement means mental competition is low for the brand. This makes this type of face asset easier to establish, and easier to keep fresh.

While initially cheaper than a celebrity, a spokesperson, if successful, can become expensive talent. For example Dean Winters, who is 'Mayhem Man' for Allstate, took home $1 million per annum for this role, as did Carly Foulkes the 'T-Mobile Girl', while Stephanie Courtney, who plays Flo from Progressive, reportedly took home $500,000 per annum (Matsuo, 2014). Therefore when thinking about a spokesperson strategy, you need to plan for success and the inevitable rise in talent costs[3].

To invest in a spokesperson as a long-term Distinctive Asset, you need to take into account that people age. As they do, their suitability for the role might also change. This is a particular concern if you use a child as a spokesperson for the brand. This could be addressed by having a stereotypical type (for example Ford's use of a brunette with a bob cut in a blue dress) where the person retains the same look, but an individual can easily be replaced with another with similar looks. Particularly, as Subway found, it is risky associating the brand with a specific person who has a name (Steinbuch, 2015).

And remember that if you decide the brand no longer wants to use that spokesperson, it is possible they may pop up elsewhere, outside your control. This happened with the former Verizon spokesperson Paul Marcarelli, who featured in advertising for Verizon's competitor, Sprint. His past role, as a spokesperson for Verizon, is explicitly acknowledged, and the advertising even uses Verizon's prior tagline 'Can you hear me now?' The efficacy of this strategy is questionable, as many people who view the advertising might find the visual presence of the same spokesperson and the audio phrase trigger Verizon alongside or instead of Sprint. For this strategy to work, the viewer needs to process a great deal of information, something that is atypical of the viewer experience when viewing advertising. Comparative advertisements are a risky strategy as these advertisements give valuable mental real estate to a competitor (Beard, 2013; Romaniuk, 2013). But comparative advertisements using a competitor's Distinctive Assets strike me as even riskier, as you give away

---

3   It is unclear what these values are based upon, as—according to Ehrenberg-Bass Institute R&D conducted in 2016—Flo is a much stronger Distinctive Asset (Fame = 74%; Uniqueness = 90%) than Mayhem Man (Fame = 28%; Uniqueness = 65%).

not just the brand, but also any advantages that Distinctive Assets confer on the brand, to a competitor.

Similarly, the Most Interesting Man in the World, fired by Dos Equis, has returned from his trip to Mars and popped up in advertising for Astral, a brand of tequila. Perhaps the only one who benefits from this is the Most Interesting Man in the World himself.

If a celebrity or a spokesperson seems too hard to manage, then the other option to develop a face for the brand is a character.

Characters

Characters are live-action or animated people, such as Ronald McDonald for McDonald's and Mama and Papa for Dolmio, or animals with human qualities, such as Aleksander the meerkat for comparethemarket.com or Monkey for PG Tips. The advantages of characters are that you have total control over their behaviour, and they don't age unless you want them to, but this approach is not without its drawbacks as animation costs can get quite expensive.

It is first useful to reflect on the history of characters and mascots, as this informs quite a bit of the current thinking on when and how to use this potential Distinctive Asset. Characters were popular in the 1950s, a nostalgic time—to both their benefit and detriment.

Characters enjoy ongoing popularity in some categories such as breakfast cereals (Tony the Tiger, Coco the Monkey) and baked goods (Sara Lee, Little Debbie and Mother, which are all represented by female characters). In these categories it is harder for any character to cut through unless it is different from others in the category. In Japan, brand characters are so ubiquitous there is even a mascot school where people can learn to be a good mascot (Telegraph, 2012).

Character-based Distinctive Assets, when common or typical for brands within a category, will struggle to build Uniqueness. This can be addressed if priority is placed on making the brand's character distinct from other characters in the category, or counter-programming the design. For example with baked goods, where most of the characters are women, developing a character that is a male would be a departure from the category's character norms.

In categories where use of characters is less common, this type of Distinctive Asset can help a brand stand out in the environment. For example take Mama and Papa for Dolmio. Hartnett (2011) included Papa in her study and he achieved 76% Fame and 94% Uniqueness, which is indicative of a strong Distinctive Asset. Much of the pasta sauce category is characterised by category norms—red and green colours, images of ingredients such as tomatoes and herbs, families having dinner, often with an Italian twist. But Dolmio, with animated characters, has Mama and Papa in advertising to help build mental availability and on pack to help with physical availability. While other brands might also have faces (for example Loyd Grossman in the UK, who is on pack and features in advertisements), none can be confused with Mama and Papa.

An example of character longevity and evolution is Louie the Fly, for insect repellent Mortein. Originating in 1957, this character has featured in many campaigns. He evolved from a simple black insect to a more person-like detailed bug, gained friends and enemies to interact with across executions, and has been killed off by the brand managers almost as often as he is killed off by Mortein[4]. If you have some time, it is instructive to see how Louie has evolved over the campaigns as a character and also the animation style (available on the company website (Mortein, 2015)).

Evidence exists that characters attract attention (Neeley & Schumann, 2004). Characters also have high Uniqueness both generally (Ward, 2017) and as pack assets (as detailed in Chapter 5). Chapter 5 revealed how characters on pack also scored highest for Fame. Further, in a comparison with celebrities and spokespeople, characters have significantly higher Fame and Uniqueness (see Figure 15.4). As a side note, spokespeople perform better on both Fame and Uniqueness than celebrities[5], which is partially the result of the lower mental competition of spokespeople.

But, despite the benefits in using characters, many marketers are reluctant to do so. I remember a conversation with a financial services brand that had a character in its brand history. A new agency had designed a multi-execution campaign that went to air, and part of it was

---

4   This is another advantage of animated characters; years of cartoons have inured us against feeling pain when a cartoon character dies!
5   Tested via ANOVA tests with post-hoc tests of significance, $p<0.05$, the database is collected from Ehrenberg-Bass Distinctive Asset studies.

Figure 15.4: A comparison of the average strength of types of faces

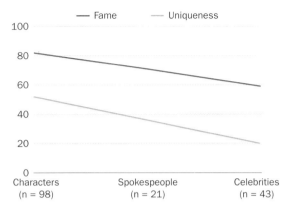

an execution that included the character cleaning the office. Guess which execution scored the highest correct branding? But the company did not want to bring back the character because it was felt the character would make the brand seem less serious.

That thinking does have some roots in truth. Metlife licensed Snoopy, the Peanuts character, more than thirty years ago in an effort to make insurance friendly to the everyday person (La Monica, 2016). But being friendly and accessible is a long way from trivialising a topic. Factors such as animation style feed into how characters can be perceived, and today's technology can lead to quite sophisticated characterisations, such as the Geico gecko, employed as brand assets in traditionally serious (or some might say boring) categories. To not draw on the brand's rich history with a character, simply because of the risk of being perceived as 'not serious', is a waste of a potentially valuable Distinctive Asset. It also overestimates the amount of thinking category buyers do (remember back to the discussion on 'projection rejection' in Chapter 7).

The biggest danger with characters is that, because people create them, effort is placed on developing the character's personality rather than its visual or audio characteristics, yet it is the visual and audio characteristics that will attract initial attention. You might create the nicest character in the world, imbued with warmth and empathy, and someone everyone would want as a friend. But, without the ability to stand out from the crowd, particularly in its facial characteristics, these personality traits will be of little value.

Another comment I have heard from people reluctant to consider investing in character assets is that characters are not relevant to millennials. This seems a bit odd given the popularity of superhero movies! The biggest issue with millennials and their acceptance of characters is that, because characters fell out of favour (like jingles), many of the re-introduced characters lack a personal history for these category buyers, so millennials might initially appear to react less positively than older category buyers who grew up with these characters. This reticence is rarely dislike, but rather due to their lack of familiarity, and so not an indicator of future character assets' (lack of) potential.

Which type of face should you choose?

Each type of face has benefits and drawbacks, and part of which type of face is the right choice for your brand is how much work you are willing to do to build the asset and how much control you want to have. Think of it like buying furniture. A celebrity is like going into a store and buying straight off the shelf; a spokesperson is like going to Ikea and getting a flat pack you have to assemble; a character is like designing what you want from scratch, and then getting a craftsperson to build it for you.

The key consideration, if your brand is going the celebrity route, is to have a plan in place to assess and overcome mental competition. If you choose the option to develop a spokesperson, plan for long-term success in both contracts and succession planning. If selecting a character, make sure your brand's asset has characteristics in the face and voice that help it stand out from the environment and also from other characters. If your brand is in a category that has high character use, counter-programming character style or focusing on a different type of asset might be the best decision to build a strong Distinctive Asset.

The next chapter moves into the realm of words, and will cover word-based assets, like taglines and fonts.

16

Taglines, Fonts and Other Word-based Assets

JENNI ROMANIUK

One type of Distinctive Asset is based around words. This asset type includes taglines or slogans ('Gives you wings'), single words ('Priceless') and the fonts in which these words are written (such as for Coca-Cola). Despite being one of the most commonly used components of brand identity, a frequent complaint is that most taglines lack memorability (Kohli, Leuthesser & Suri, 2007). For example in a test of brand attribution for thirty slogans for major US brands, only three slogans scored higher than 50% correct brand linkage (Kiley, 2004).

A rose by any other name . . .

Words are stored in our semantic memory, which stores words and meanings (Tulving, 1972). Our understanding of what each word means comes from the other thoughts we have attached to that word in our memory. Most of the time, our understanding of what a word means occurs subconsciously. This process becomes explicit when we try to learn another language. If you are an English speaker, and you start to learn Spanish, you first learn to associate a Spanish word with the English word, and then all the meanings attached to that English word. For example *vino* becomes attached to 'wine'. When someone asks you '*¿Quieres un vaso de vino?*' your memory breaks this down to 'Would you like a glass of wine?', which evokes the associations you have for wine, and you then use these thoughts to formulate your answer.

These additional steps take cognitive effort and time, not long in actual seconds, but much longer than if someone asks you the same question in your native language. But as you get familiar with this new word, *vino* creates direct attachments to the concepts that define its meaning, removing that extra cognitive step in memory. As a consequence your responses become quicker, automatic, fluent.

Just as Spanish, Chinese and Russian each give you a new word for wine (*vino*, 红酒 and Вино respectively), a tagline asset can give you new words for the brand. But as a new tagline often comprises prior known words, these words, unless made up like 'Drinkability' for Bud Light, typically have other (non–brand name) meanings that compete with the brand name for retrieval.

Indeed, taglines are often chosen for richness in meaning, and how this could contribute to the brand's image or attitude (Dahlén & Rosengren, 2005). For example in a recent interview, Helmut Meysenburg, Head of Strategies at BMW stated the tagline 'sheer driving pleasure' was chosen to communicate the joy about the car and mobility (Groeppel-Klein, 2014). As with any other asset, if the meaning is too rich, this additional mental competition can hamper asset building.

The benefits of taglines/word based assets

Taglines have executional advantages over other assets. This type of asset can be spoken or written, which provides higher multi-platform adaptability than most other assets. Any medium with a visual or audio component can include a tagline. Taglines are also flexible to execute within an advertisement, as the words can be shown, spoken, sung; be moving or static text and so on. These benefits can make a tagline a valuable addition to any Distinctive Asset palette. But the drawback of a tagline asset is that—because taglines are of a form similar to the brand name (comprising words)—this asset type does not add neurological diversity to branding options. Words will also have reduced capacity to cut through when the media environment is also word-rich, such as in newspapers.

The tagline ingredients that drive Fame and Uniqueness

The general execution factors that build the strength of a Distinctive Asset—reach, co-presentation and consistency—also apply when building a strong tagline asset. But choosing a brand-smart tagline can give the brand a head start for a strong tagline asset. Prior research has focused on the memorability of the tagline itself, such as how many people, when asked to think of taglines, think of the 'You're in good hands' phrase, irrespective of any links to Allstate Insurance (such as in Kohli, Thomas & Suri, 2013). As our interest is in taglines as Distinctive Assets, the paramount concern is the strength of the link between the tagline *and* the brand name.

The components of a tagline

When constructing a tagline or choosing between alternatives, what are the factors of a taglines' composition (such as length, nature of words, rhymes) that help or hinder tagline Fame or Uniqueness? The next piece of research addresses this question.

The data comprise 209 taglines from five predominantly English-speaking countries (the USA, the UK, Australia, New Zealand and South Africa). English-speaking countries were the focus because some variables involve looking at the rarity of words[1] and this was only available for the English language[2]. The taglines spanned brands from packaged goods, services and durable categories. These measurements were collected as part of our fundamental R&D or contracted commercial research, and each drew from a sample of buyers for the category of interest (typically around 400 to 600 respondents in each study).

Fame and Uniqueness were measured and calculated in line with the approaches discussed in Chapters 9 and 10. Across the taglines included there is considerable variation in both metrics, which is useful when

---

1   Davies's (n.d.) *Word and phrase: info* is the site used to determine the rarity of words in taglines. It has rank scores for 60,000 English words. In the case of multiple uses or meanings, the lowest-ranked score is used for modelling.

2   It would be great to replicate this analysis in other languages; any researchers who are interested, do let me know as I have a database of taglines that could be used for this purpose.

modelling: average tagline Fame was 30%, ranging from 2% to 88%; while average Uniqueness was 68%, ranging from 5% to 99%.

The factors

The factors modelled include the length of the tagline, the rarity of words used, the inclusion of the brand name, a 'generic' product category or price reference, and some rhetorical devices—such as rhyme, a question structure or audio enhancers—used in taglines (for more on these devices, see Miller & Toman, 2016). Table 16.1 lists the full set of factors, how they were measured and descriptive statistics for the data set.

Most of these factors were hypothesised as linked to higher Fame or Uniqueness. The exception is direct reference to the category or price, which represents generic messages that could be confused with other brands and so could result in lower Uniqueness. These variables were modelled first with single linear regressions to test for individual relationships and to check the multivariate model did not distort results. The next stage involved a multiple linear regression, to test the combined and individual capacity of the factors to estimate the Fame and Uniqueness scores for each tagline.

Table 16.1: Key analysis variables for tagline composition

Factor	Description	Hypothesis	Example	Study descriptives
Length	Number of words in the tagline	The longer the tagline, the less famous but more unique it would be	'Open happiness' (2 words)	Average number of words = 4 Range from 1 to 14 words
Rarest word	The frequency rank of the most uncommon word	The inclusion of a rarer word, leads to higher Fame and higher Uniqueness	'Mayhem everywhere' *Mayhem* (rarest) = 12,662 everywhere = 1948	Average rarest = 5759 Range from 4 to 60,000 (max in database)
Lead-word rarity	The rarity of the first word in the tagline	The rarer the first word, the higher the Fame and Uniqueness of the tagline	'Keep walking' *Keep* (first) = rank 156 *Walking* = rank 3661	Average across taglines = 1770 Range from 1 to 60,000

Factor	Description	Hypothesis	Example	Study descriptives
Brand name	If the brand name is a normal part of the tagline	The inclusion of the brand name will lead to higher Fame and Uniqueness	'Share a Coke and a song'	14% of taglines included the brand name Higher in beverages and durables (around 30%)
Generic category or price reference	If the category or major category benefit is part of the tagline	The inclusion of the category will lead to lower Uniqueness but not affect Fame	'Expert care for damaged *hair*'	35% of taglines included direct mention of the product category or price
Rhyme	Is a rhyming device used?	A rhyming device will lead to higher Uniqueness but not affect Fame	'Don't get mad, get Glad'	7% of taglines included a rhyming element No difference across categories
Audio enhancement	Is there an audio device such as music, sonic or a rhythm of speaking?	Audio enhancement will lead to higher Uniqueness but not affect Fame	'Snap! Crackle! Pop!' (with music accompaniment)	11% of taglines had some form of audio enhancement Higher amongst durables (44%)
Question	Is the tagline in the form of a question?	Framing the tagline as a question will lead to higher Fame and Uniqueness.	'Can you hear me now?'	3% of taglines were in the form of a question Tended to be in food categories (8%)

Both multivariate regression models were statistically significant and explained 21% of variance in Fame scores and 15% of the variance in Uniqueness scores[3]. There were similarities and differences in the key factors for each metric. The results are summarised in Figure 16.1.

---

3   Adjusted R^2 values, $p<0.001$ for both models.

Figure 16.1: Tagline component factors that could impact Fame or Uniqueness or both

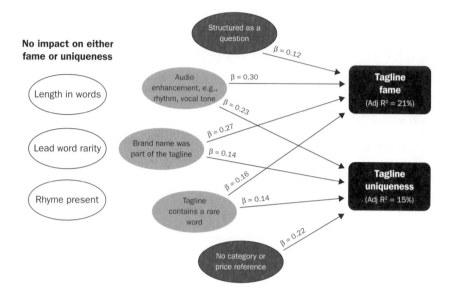

Summary of results

Three factors are linked to both higher Fame and Uniqueness:

- *audio enhancement*—this involves some form of music or rhythm in how the tagline is vocalised.
- *brand name*—this is including the brand name in the tagline at least when building up the asset (it can be removed later). While significant for both metrics, it had around double the influence on Fame as on Uniqueness.
- *rare word*—this is including an unusual word in the tagline, a word that stands out.

Of the factors related to either Fame or Uniqueness, having the tagline posing a question also has a positive relationship with Fame. But the presence of a generic category or price reference was detrimental to Uniqueness.

Finally, the factors that do not affect either Fame or Uniqueness are the length of the tagline, lead-word rarity and the use of rhyme.

So when creating or selecting a tagline, it is useful to remember these points.

It's not what you say, but how you say it: audio enhancement

Length didn't matter, neither did rhyme; but audio enhancements, such as rhythm, tone, music and vocal characteristics, had a positive impact on tagline Distinctive Asset strength. The findings for length do conflict with the traditional maxim of 'keep it simple' as suggested by Kohli and colleagues (2013). This is because prior research focused on the memorability of the slogan, whereas our interest here is in the *memorability of the brand name in situations when the slogan is present.*

Other research shows consumers don't dislike long taglines (Dass et al., 2014), but the longer a tagline is, the harder it is to remember. If your interest is in using the tagline as a messaging device, then memorability of that message is important, and it is in your interest to keep it short. But when considering memorability of the brand in the context of the slogan, other factors play a greater role and these might require length to be achieved or can make a longer tagline easier to develop. Rather than trying to reduce length, think about how to create a tagline that rolls off the tongue and is easy to say (see Chapter 17, which discusses sound and music assets, and explores this in detail).

Fill in the . . . : brand name

Incorporating the brand in the tagline helps build links to the brand, as people mentally fill in the silence or blank space with the brand name. Incorporating the brand fast-tracks co-presentation in the early stages of asset development. But, while this might be unsurprising, there is a danger you can draw on something too common. Sometimes a tagline comprises a well-known phrase that happen to incorporate a brand name, such as 'The Citi never sleeps' for Citibank. This would seem like an obvious choice to use. The danger with appropriating a common phrase that naturally incorporates the brand, however, is that the phrase is processed holistically, rather than as a set of individual words— which is the processing needed to recognise that one of these words is a brand name. This type of tagline asset often has high Uniqueness, with competitor attribution rare, but it typically underperforms Fame expectations.

In a few examples we have tested, the Fame scores were around 40%, even when the tagline being tested actually contains the brand name and the brand name has 100% awareness! If you are considering appropriating a common phrase for a brand, use visual and audio devices to clearly separate the brand name from the rest of the phrase.

The power of word rarity

Including an unusual word can help a tagline have higher Fame and Uniqueness, so be creative with language. An example of this is Specsavers and their use of 'Should've' (Padmore, 2016). By creating a new word or including an uncommon word, a tagline or phrase is boosted in memorability, similar to how brand names composed of rare words are encoded with greater clarity (Meyers-Levy, 1989).

Avoid the generic

The one negative result of reference to the product category or price leading to lower Uniqueness is also worthy of further discussion. Having a tagline that references the category or price should have a natural advantage of wider relevance. But this relevance comes at a branding cost—it is harder to own this tagline. As these types of taglines often change to follow current trends, this heightens the danger of convergence with other brands (as discussed in Chapter 7). For example during the financial crisis all supermarket taglines emphasised low prices—such as Walmart's 'Always low prices' and 'Save money live better'; and Kroger's 'More value for the way you live' and 'Low prices plus more'. Therefore, when formulating your tagline to become a Distinctive Asset (rather than a messaging device, which can be more current and transient), think less about current relevance and focus on memorability and longevity.

Font assets

Everything written down has to have some form of font. Fun fact—the first computer font was called 'Digi Grotesk' and designed by a German inventor, Rudolph Hell, for his cathode-ray typesetting machines (see Figure 16.2).

Figure 16.2: The first computer font—Digi Grotesk

First computer font

Font is a fixed quality similar to colour but, while everything needs to be written in a font, we often don't process the font as a separate entity (similar to how we process colour). It is only when a font characteristic is called out as a separate feature of design that we notice specific font qualities. In general, when compared to other assets, although the lack of cut-through means Fame scores are often low, it is rare for the fonts tested as Distinctive Assets to be confused with other brands[4], and so they typically score high in Uniqueness. An illustration of this is in Figure 16.3, which shows results for the IBM font, across four countries[5].

Figure 16.3: IBM font Fame and Uniqueness metrics across four countries

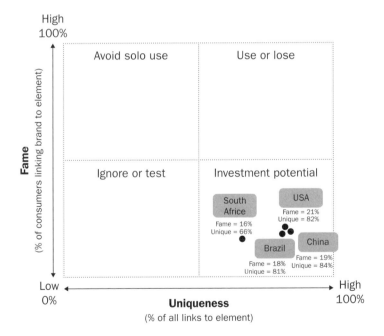

---

4 It is important to acknowledge the selection bias here; we only include fonts that have been identified as possible Distinctive Assets and so tend to be either proprietary or stylistically different in some way. Many brand fonts are not intended to be Distinctive Assets, and these fonts will have lower Uniqueness.

5 Ehrenberg-Bass Institute R&D online survey, $n = 600$ in each country, 2014.

A drawback of font assets is that the visual presence of the word is necessary to convey the font. The main thing the font has in its favour is its use on pack, as well as in e-commence and m-commerce. If the brand can build a font asset and it can be prominently executed in retail environments, the added benefits to building physical availability may therefore be sufficient to overcome other executional limitations.

A good example of building a font as a Distinctive Asset is Snickers, when the brand replaces the word *Snickers* on pack with other relevant words such as *hungry*. The building of this font asset was enhanced by the separation of the font from brand that featured in above-the-line advertising such as billboards, as well as in-store on the product's packaging.

The next chapter focuses on audio assets, such as voices, music and sounds.

17

Developing a 'sound' strategy

JENNI ROMANIUK

In its heyday, radio was the age of deep, resonant voices, jingles and alliteration, designed to be pleasurable and memorable for the ears in an environment often plagued by distraction. Sound was used creatively, but also as a branding tool. With the advent of television, the eyes took over. We started designing to please the eyes first, with the focus on visual images, and the ears second. Sound became a creative device to further the visual story, to set the mood, and be a support act rather than a separate sensory device.

Then advertising, like the Cadbury Gorilla advertisement, shifted the pendulum to the other direction, where the music became an integral part of the creative effort. Advertisements leveraged catchy songs to grab attention and stimulate emotions (Binet, Müllensiefen & Edwards, 2013). The role of sound as *a branding device* was often downgraded; for example Romaniuk (2009) reported that the average number of times the brand is spoken in a television advertisement is lower than the brand's visual frequency. Take the time to review the advertising over a normal night of television and you will see how many advertisements don't even verbalise the brand name at all.

Recent technological advances, such as the growth of mobile communication and the expansion of digital streaming services, such as Spotify or podcasts, herald a resurgence in sound-dominant advertising media (even though listening to current podcast advertising reminds me of the old-style radio announcer endorsements, with awkward segues from the programming to promote the charms of the product or service of the moment). And let us not forget, radio didn't die; it is still a major part of people's lives, particularly those who commute. Nielsen (2016) reported the reach of radio in the USA was higher than television or smartphones, while OfCom reports 64% of the UK population and 78% of the German population listen to the radio regularly (OfCom, 2015).

This chapter takes an in-depth look at Distinctive Assets that are audio based, and how to select and use these assets. The chapter has particular relevance for marketers looking to construct a Distinctive Asset palette, as audio assets tend to be the most common type of asset missing.

The power of sound

Some sounds have attention-grabbing power. We become programmed for certain sounds to cut through in the environment[1]. Examples of sounds that cut through include our own name, referred to as the cocktail-party effect, or our own phone ringing, both of which we notice, even in a cacophony. This heightened awareness is not innate but rather something we become trained to notice over time. A quick illustration of this is when you change your ring tone on your phone: for a time after the change it takes a few rings for your brain to register it is your phone, but after a while you become attuned to notice, and respond to, the new sound.

Second, certain sounds, such as music or certain vocal timbres, can affect our emotions and responsiveness to the situation. On poker machines, the sounds the machine makes when someone has won are designed to evoke a pleasure response, while a plumbing company made great use of the annoyance that the sound of a dripping tap generates to get the listeners'

---

1   This is referred to as a 'bottom-up' attention grab, because it comes from our subconscious mind and reaches our conscious brain; contrasted with 'top-down' attention that starts with our conscious thoughts seeking something specific.

attention at the start of their radio ads (yes, Metropolitan Plumbing, I still remember you!). Certain songs can take us back on a mental journey to our childhood, love or heartbreak, and other key moments in our lives.

Audio Distinctive Assets can make two contributions. First, these assets can attract attention to the brand, as part of the advertising experience, in audio-only media environments. Second, audio assets can extend the reach of the brand in multi-mode media, such as television, so people not giving visual attention to the advertisement can still notice the brand. Both of these benefits are predicated on the capacity of the sound Distinctive Asset to compete for attention with other stimuli present in the environment (including other sounds), and for the brand to be the salient memory evoked when the sound is experienced[2].

Audio assets come in two broad types: ones that are related to sounds, and ones relating to music.

An orchestra of sound assets

Sound assets are non-musical noises that can signal the brand in advertising with an audio component. These include non-vocal sounds, vocal sounds and style components.

Non-vocal sounds

Non-vocal sound assets are created noises that become linked to the brand, such as the Intel inside sound or the McCain's 'ping'. These noises attract attention by providing audio punctuation for a key moment, or as a sign-off for an advertisement. Not all attention-grabbing sounds are branding devices—for example a phone ring or even silence can grab someone's attention—but this will not act as a brand trigger unless a link with the brand is present in listeners' memories.

Often non-vocal sounds can struggle to achieve high brand linkage. In a piece of R&D into Distinctive Assets in the telecommunications category in the USA, we assessed the strength of AT&T's and T-Mobile's audio

---

2   Also remember the brand name can be spoken out loud. This is often a neglected brand
     execution tactic!

sign-offs[3]. While AT&T (Fame = 19%, Uniqueness = 62%) scored higher than T-Mobile (Fame = 3%, Uniqueness = 33%), despite widespread use of these sign-offs in television advertisements, neither was even close to being a usable Distinctive Asset. Figure 17.2 shows how non-vocal sounds generally tend to underperform relative to other audio assets.

Vocal sounds

Vocal sounds are any audio assets made with the human voice. This can be a voice, a tone or other human sounds like laughter or a cough. Voices can be attached to a specific person, a character or just a voice-over. Some well-known people have unique voices (for example James Earl Jones), and the danger with this is the same as a celebrity face—you are distracted by who is speaking and so fail to process what is spoken (the brand).

A study into the US insurance category in 2015 tested both the visual images of characters, spokesmodels and celebrities, and audio recordings of their voices[4]. The assets tested included the Geico gecko, Flo from Progressive, Dennis Haysbert from Allstate and the Box character from Progressive (whose voice is provided by Chris Parnell from *Saturday Night Live*). In each case, the voice and visual assets are used separately, such as in the voice-over at the start of an advertisement, before the character/person appears, as well as in combination.

As Figure 17.1 shows, while the pairs of visual and audio assets (for example Flo image and Flo voice; or the Box image and the Box voice) had similar Uniqueness levels, the visual images had much higher (by 20–40 percentage points) Fame scores than their audio counterparts. However, voices can be stronger than visual assets, as evident in the gecko voice scoring more highly than the visual of the Box character.

Vocal tones can also affect the interpretation of the spoken word. If people raise their voice at the end of a sentence, this is decoded as them asking a question or expressing doubt in their own comments, while we find deep, resonant tones trustworthy, due to the link between the capacity to produce these sounds, chest size and the corresponding ability to

---

3   An online survey in 2016 with 300 respondents aged 18+ years.
4   Source: Ehrenberg-Bass Institute online study, 2015 *n* = 300.

Figure 17.1: Comparison of audio voices and visual assets in the US insurance industry

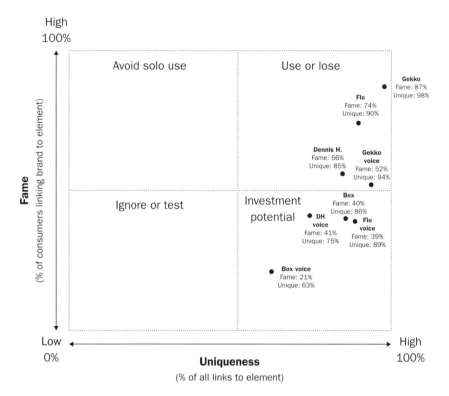

protect us from danger (for example Klofstad, Anderson & Peters, 2012). But while tone can convey meaning, for a vocal sound to be a Distinctive Asset, it needs sufficient individuality that it can be attached to one brand only. This puts a premium on unusual voices or accents for vocal assets.

Style components

Different acoustic styles can be used to develop audio Distinctive Assets. One example of style creation is to have a rhythm, as in Mastercard's Priceless campaign, where the words change but the rhythm of expression (number of syllables, pause presence and length) stays the same across executions. This approach can work due to our tendency to notice and respond to patterns—we mentally move with the rhythm of the conversation.

A symphony of music assets

Music is integrated into advertising in a variety of ways, and some of these ways can be used as branding devices. While music can generate an emotional response, this is not the focus of this section, except to the extent the emotion generated helps or hinders the music's capacity to act as an effective branding device. Musical devices come in three basic forms: jingles, popular songs and background music.

Jingles

Jingles are original musical pieces with brand-based lyrics—the Big Mac ingredient song and the Oscar Mayer song are two examples, and chances are, for those of you in the USA, these jingles are easy to recall, even after a long absence. Reflecting my own Australian childhood memories, I didn't realise I held the entire song for Arnott's Yo-Yo biscuits in my brain until my niece asked me to describe these biscuits (d0nkeyshines, 2011). As jingles are created for the brand, they come with little, if any, mental competition. The combination of the power of music to encourage memorisation and the integration of the brand name also enhances the co-presentation qualities. These characteristics are the building blocks for a strong Distinctive Asset, and indeed some are heralding that it is now time for the return of the jingle (Taylor, 2015).

Popular songs

Popular songs can be adopted as branding devices. Sometimes the choice is due to an obvious link such as Shout cleaning products and the song 'Shout', or California Raisins and 'Heard It Through The Grapevine'. Other times a popular song can be used with a modified lyric designed to fit in with the need of the commercial, such as Cadbury and the Beach Boys song 'Wouldn't It Be Nice', or back in the 1980s, McDonald's repurposing the song 'Mac The Knife' to be sung by the character Mac Tonight (OffbeatFrontier, 2010).

Popular songs are like musical celebrities in that they can suffer from mental competition due to the associative networks already present in the brain (for example the artist or personal memories). This creates the risk that the song, like a celebrity, will overwhelm the brand, and hamper memorability. People will remember the song but not the brand that brought it to them.

Popular music also risks wearing out, so that people will switch off or take active steps avoid advertising. Advertising schedules, often involving repeat exposure in a short period of time, exacerbates this wear-out. Therefore, when thinking of music as a branding device, ask yourself—can I see the brand using this song for the next twenty years? If yes, then by all means go through the work to establish it as a branding device. If not, then just consider its value as a creative cost, and use other Distinctive Assets and the brand name for branding.

Chou and Lien (2010) provide evidence that, since we form our music preferences as teenagers, listening to music from this time as we age can evoke positive memories. Drawing on this finding, Major, Romaniuk and Nenycz-Thiel (2012) tested if this positive emotion carried through to memorability, to see if popular songs were more memorably linked to the brand advertising amongst those who were teenagers when the songs were released. The results showed that brand linkage was not linked to the age of the category buyer but rather to current music consumption levels. People who listen to a lot of music are more likely to remember any musical assets than people who rarely listen to music. This means designing the branding for ears that like to listen to music, rather than the person attached to those ears.

Background music

These are commissioned pieces of instrumental music that play in the background. While this music has the advantage of little or no mental competition to hamper the brand becoming attached, it often lacks the prominence or the co-presentation to quickly become a strong branding asset. Major and colleagues (2012) found, when comparing brand linkage for different types of music, that background music was significantly lower than jingles or popular music.

But this type of music can be cultivated over time, and permeate the subconscious. I realised the power of background music when I turned on the television in the USA to a typical car advertisement, with a car driving down a generic street somewhere—but something triggered Mazda in my brain. Now there was no external reason why Mazda should be salient: I have never owned a Mazda and, while I am aware of the brand, I have no strong positive or negative feelings. There were no obvious brand triggers such as a distinct style of car or even 'Zoom Zoom'. The source of the brand trigger (after much googling of Mazda advertisements in different countries) turned out to be that same background music.

The link between this music and the Mazda was not at a conscious level, as I didn't even remember the music as a feature of the advertisement, but at a subconscious level. It is unfortunate that my subconscious won't tell me how many exposures it took to create this link—but I suspect quite a few.

Which types of audio assets are stronger?

To explore if evidence exists that some types of audio assets perform better than others, we drew on a database of 127 audio assets that were selected for testing by brand managers and agencies for brands in ten categories. Fame and Uniqueness scores were collected as part of category-specific studies into Distinctive Asset strength. The audio assets were divided into five categories: jingles, background music, popular songs, vocal sounds and non-vocal sounds.

The results of ANOVA tests reveal (Figure 17.2) popular songs and jingles have similar levels of Fame, but non-vocal sounds are significantly lower[5]. In Uniqueness, jingles outperform other assets, and again non-vocal sounds score significantly lower[6].

But a review of the performance scores within asset types reveals a wide variance, so while jingles may on average score better than other assets, most types had assets in the use-or-lose quadrant and in the ignore-or-test quadrant. As Figure 17.3 shows, the majority of audio assets tested fell into the investment-potential quadrant (58%), with 31% in ignore or test, and 11% in use or lose. To give these figures context, the comparative figures from the tagline database (from Chapter 16) are

---

5   Outcome of Games-Howell post-hoc significance tests, $p = 0.041$ significantly lower than for
      popular songs (Games-Howell chosen due to failure to pass homogeneity of variance tests).
6   Outcome of Bonferroni significance tests, $p = 0.012$ significantly lower than for jingles.

Figure 17.2: Relative performance of audio asset types

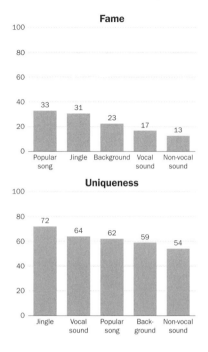

Fame

Popular song	33
Jingle	31
Background	23
Vocal sound	17
Non-vocal sound	13

Uniqueness

Jingle	72
Vocal sound	64
Popular song	62
Background	59
Non-vocal sound	54

Figure 17.3: Performance distribution of audio assets by sub-type

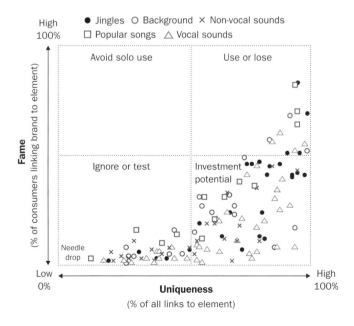

High 100% ● Jingles ○ Background ✕ Non-vocal sounds
□ Popular songs △ Vocal sounds

Fame (% of consumers linking brand to element)

Avoid solo use · Use or lose

Ignore or test · Investment potential

Needle drop

Low 0% · Uniqueness · High 100%
(% of all links to element)

55% with investment potential, 22% in ignore or test, and 23% in use or lose. Taglines have twice the number of usable assets as audio assets. This underscores the challenges in building audio-based assets, and the relative rarity with which strong assets of this type are achieved.

That brings us to the end of the chapters on specific assets types. The next chapter shows how to set up a Distinctive Asset management system, to identify, build, monitor and protect a brand's Distinctive Assets.

18

Creating a Distinctive Asset Management System

JENNI ROMANIUK

Building strong Distinctive Assets is not a one-time task but an ongoing process. This chapter outlines how to develop a system to develop, maintain and protect your brand's Distinctive Assets over the longer term.

The five-stage plan

Figure 18.1 illustrates five stages to set up a system for managing Distinctive Assets. The first two stages identify the priorities and clear away barriers, and the remaining three stages are designed to create an ongoing information-and-feedback loop to meet the brand's current and future Distinctive Asset needs.

Figure 18.1: The Distinctive Asset management system

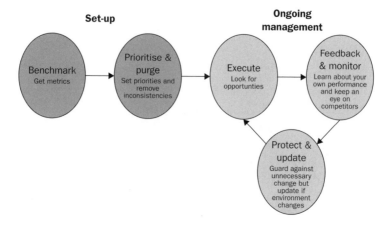

Stage 1: Benchmark

The first stage is to benchmark to determine which current assets have the potential to be used or developed further. While the three steps in this stage typically provide a reality check for all involved, they also create the objective facts for everyone to draw on for future Distinctive Asset decisions.

Identify potential assets

The first step is to identify assets for testing in the benchmark study. Potential sources of knowledge about assets include current and past stakeholders, such as brand managers, insights, creative agencies, design agencies, even the CEO—anyone with a role in how the brand is presented to the world. Where possible, involve past stakeholders who might identify forgotten assets that could be resurrected.

It is also useful to engage an independent person to review the brand's material, as this can detect unintentionally consistent or prominent assets. For example we identified a brand's background music as consistent, something the current brand management team was unaware of, and the agency staff had forgotten. This turned out to be an investable asset for the brand, one that would have been missed without independent review.

In the benchmarking stage, err on the side of including any potential asset to the extent that is feasible for data collection. This avoids missed opportunities and helps all stakeholder voices to feel heard. For a global brand, it is important to ask local offices for input at this point in time, as they have detailed insights into local campaigns and competitors that might also reveal asset opportunities or challenges.

Review competitors' material

The next step is to look for potential competitors' assets, so these can be incorporated into the benchmark study. The performance of competitors has an influence on these two factors:

- *strategic imperative*—Chapter 10 revealed how categories vary in the number of strong assets. If competitors have many strong assets, Distinctive Assets are a category hygiene factor needed to become or remain competitive, and so speedy investment is required.
- *location and number of no-go zones*—these are areas to avoid as competitors are stronger in these assets or asset types, and so the potential for confusion and misattribution is high. For example if a competitor is strong for a comedic advertising style, then you can avoid introducing a similar style.

Quantitative measurement

The final step in Stage 1 is to put numbers to the relative strength of these assets, and use the Distinctive Asset grid to plot each asset's future potential. The assets that are usable or that have investment potential will form the main pool of assets for the next stage: prioritise and purge.

Stage 2: Prioritise and purge

There are just two steps in this stage, as its name suggests: setting priorities and getting rid of (purging) inconsistencies.

Set priorities

The first step is to choose the brand's priority assets. The common grid formations and actions discussed in Chapter 11 provide guidance, tailored to your current position, on how to prioritise. It is useful to involve creative and media agencies at this stage, to provide input into the creative possibilities that potential assets generate, including their use across media platforms. It is rare for only one possible path to emerge at this stage, so be prepared to have to make choices.

If the brand's starting point has no usable or investable assets, then draw on the brand's operating environments to help to identify assets that, if developed, have the best potential to influence both mental and physical availability. At the same time, still take heed of competitors' results and avoid areas where competitors are strong. Why make a challenge even more difficult by unnecessarily mimicking competitors?

When setting the number of assets to prioritise, tackle your asset building in waves. That is, build the first wave of assets to be strong and, only after that has been achieved, move onto the second wave. This helps to focus attention and resources on a smaller number of priorities at one time. If you have a small advertising or promotion budget, pick one asset to be the focus for the next year. If the brand has a substantive budget, still focus on only a few assets, and aim to build these assets quickly. Trying to build many assets at the same time leads to a lack of executional focus, as it becomes difficult to fit all of the necessary prominent co-presentation moments into each touch-point.

Remember: it is better to have one asset at the 100% Fame, 100% Uniqueness level than more assets with only investment potential.

The inconsistency purge

Once you have identified the priority assets, the final step of Stage 2 is to review all the brand's material and remove any asset-execution inconsistencies. Remember to look widely, through all digital, in-store, internal and external company material. Everything from the annual report to employment advertisements to internal forms—wherever that priority asset might be used.

Think of it as a general spring clean of your brand's assets. Remove all of the inconsistencies as quickly as possible, irrespective of the extent of difference. This will avoid handicapping future asset-building activities.

Stage 3: Execute

Get past inconsistencies back on track

The first step is to re-execute the inconsistencies identified in the purge stage, so they are in line with your asset-building objectives. This is to convert past barriers to a strong Distinctive Asset, into helpers.

Look for new execution opportunities

The next step is to identify new opportunities where the brand's priority Distinctive Assets can be included. While the focus is on executing the Distinctive Assets, don't neglect the brand name. First, you need the brand name to anchor the new memories of Distinctive Assets (as described in Chapter 2). Second, depending on the brand's Distinctive Asset palette, sometimes the brand name will be the best execution option. For example the absence of an audio Distinctive Asset doesn't mean you need to neglect audio branding. Having the brand name spoken aloud can still cut through to those who do not have eyes on a screen.

These three Ps provide a useful checklist for reviewing each piece of communication:

- *presence*—which assets are we using? If none, can we introduce an asset?
- *prominence*—is the asset a noticeable part of the communications? Is there anything we can do to improve its prominence?
- *(co)presentation*—is the asset close enough to the brand name that a viewer experiences both the asset and the brand at the same time (in the same visual or audio moment)?

Review your brand's past media and creative efforts. Check that the brand's media plans aim to reach all category buyers (see Romaniuk, 2016c, for why reach planning should be integral to your media strategy) and that the creative work appeals to all category buyers. Neglecting any category-buying segment will put a ceiling on your Distinctive Asset–building potential. If, as described in Chapter 9, you have large customer segments for whom the asset has lower Fame scores, revamp your media or creative planning or both to fix this imbalance.

How long does it take to build up an asset?

The length of time it will take a brand to build up an asset depends on the broadness of the asset-building reach, and how much attention these activities attract within each environment. Assets can be built quite quickly if investment results in a substantial increase in reach, but often growth comes via a steady improvement as cumulative reach takes time to build (Sharp, Riebe & Nelson-Field, 2013). The asset's Fame scores should steadily increase as asset-building activities reach a greater number of category buyers, while still maintaining freshness amongst those with existing asset-brand links. It won't happen overnight . . .

Stage 4: Feedback and monitor

This stage takes place once you have started your Distinctive Asset–building activities.

Obtain some feedback

The first step is to obtain feedback on the performance of your own asset-building activities, while also keeping an eye on competitors' activities. A minimum of six months to roll out substantively new asset-building activities is typical; a follow-up twelve months after benchmarking allows enough time to pass so that the brand's efforts could have widespread effect. Occasionally an interim six-month follow-up can be useful, if changes were quick and implementation wide. You will find little value in tracking Distinctive Asset strength every month or even every quarter.

Keep an eye on competitors

Uniqueness is an essential quality for a strong Distinctive Asset, and the one you have the least control over. It is therefore useful to monitor competitor activities to look for changes in asset prominence, copying or any new asset introductions.

Retail settings are very competitive environments, and if your competitors have greater cut-through then it is likely to be at your brand's expense. Educate and use sales staff to keep an eye on Distinctive Assets being used in a retail setting, to detect changes early. This way you can, where necessary, quickly retaliate by ramping up your brand's in-store Distinctive Asset presence.

Stage 5: Protect and update

Protect at all costs

Once your brand has strong Distinctive Assets, it becomes important to protect them, with an eye to sensibly updating these assets when circumstances warrant. The first step is to learn to say *'No!'* to suggestions on how Distinctive Assets can be improved, as it is rare that these suggestions are helpful.

Distinctive Assets do have natural managerial predators who swoop down and make 'improvement' suggestions that will damage your Distinctive Asset–building strategy. Here are three such predators to watch out for, and suggestions on how to deal with them, if you are directly confronted:

- *the short-attention-span manager*—this is the manager who gets easily bored with the status quo and wants to change things, to 'keep it fresh'. They can be identified by their over-attachment to their phone or smartwatch, which they use to keep themselves entertained in any meeting that lasts longer than ten minutes. To protect your assets from this type of manager, it can be useful to distract them by always having something new to highlight that is unrelated to Distinctive Assets. That way they can feel excited by the change, and you can keep the Distinctive Assets from their focus.
- *the 'disruptor' manager*—this is the manager who dreams of disruption and so wants to do things differently, just to be different. This manager can be identified by the picture of Elon Musk in their wallet, and their constant mantra of 'What would Uber do?' If confronted with this Distinctive Asset predator point out that, in times of rapid change, *not* changing Distinctive Assets is the most disruptive move you can make. This should confuse them for sufficient time for you to quickly exit.
- *the shiny-new-thing manager*—this is the manager who wants to incorporate the latest in media, technology, anything. This type of manager usually identifies themselves with the call to show you their new gadget, app, tracker etc. The best approach to tackling this type

of predator is to ask their opinion on how to incorporate Distinctive Assets into some form of new technology. As they focus on sharing their own opinion and the wonders of the new technology, they are distracted from commenting specifically on the Distinctive Asset.

Assets don't have to stay frozen in time, but do think evolution rather than revolution when it comes to change. You will get pressure to change, update or refresh assets. Resist this pressure. Give anyone with helpful suggestions this book to read and then say you will only discuss their ideas after that. These are the most common times when there will be direct or indirect pressure to change assets:

- a new brand manager
- a new marketing manager
- a new CEO
- a decline in market share/sales
- a new advertising campaign
- a new advertising agency
- a new media platform
- a new distribution channel.

Some of these triggers, such as a new media platform or distribution channel, are good opportunities to review the asset list to determine any gaps where a new asset or evolution of an existing asset might bolster brand execution quality in that environment. The others are not necessarily reasons to change assets, but may require you to educate key stakeholders as to why consistency is imperative. Protection is a major component of being the custodian of a brand's Distinctive Assets.

The final short chapter covers the four principles or 'commandments' you should remember to keep your Distinctive Asset–building activities on track.

19

The Four Commandments for Building Distinctive Assets

JENNI ROMANIUK

We started with the seven costly sins, so let's finish with the four commandments for building strong Distinctive Assets: which are the key principles to always keep in mind.

Figure 19.1: The Four Commandments

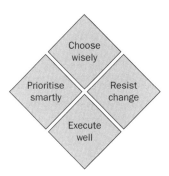

Commandment 1: Choose wisely

Building strong Distinctive Assets is difficult; don't handicap yourself by selecting poorly. Avoid assets with pre-existing mental competition, such as linkages to competitors or strong non-brand meanings. Don't abandon usable assets or even ones with investment potential, where the brand might have a head start, without a strong, evidence-based reason. Remember: if you (or category buyers) are bored with an asset, that just means you need better creative content.

Choose wisely when you are thinking of adding to the Distinctive Asset palette. There are two questions to ask yourself in this situation:

- what does this give the brand that other assets are unable to provide?
- will building this asset still leave sufficient resources to protect existing assets?

The asset's exclusive contribution

An additional, similar asset is an unnecessary distraction. To make an asset worthy of long-term investment, it should, at minimum, provide the brand with additional flexibility, adaptability or neurological diversity.

Resource allocation

You need to have the money and attention to add another asset. If you fragment the brand's resources too much, existing assets can be left vulnerable. Protection of existing strong assets should always be a priority, so always consider the vulnerabilities that might be created by spending on developing a new asset rather than reinforcing an existing asset.

Commandment 2: Prioritise smartly

Don't try to build too many assets at once. Remember that the goal is to move an asset to close to 100% Fame and 100% Uniqueness, and that having one asset here is worth ten with investment potential. This means setting realistic goals about the number of assets to build in the next year and committing to these assets first. If you tackle building the whole Distinctive Asset palette in waves, over time the process becomes easier, as building a strong Distinctive Asset gives the brand another anchor to help build the next Distinctive Asset.

Commandment 3: Execute well

Valuable assets are known by all category buyers. This will happen with greater speed if the execution is wide and prominent, aimed at reaching all category buyers. Many assets languish in the background, not attracting the attention they need to affect category buyers' memories. Often these assets are placed too far away from the brand to easily form linkages. Assets need attention *and* anchoring with the brand to be built.

Even a strong asset needs to build brand linkages amongst new category buyers. While a strong asset can be used without the brand for existing buyers, it still needs to reach out to new category buyers with asset-building activities, which need to involve the brand name. These asset-building activities can also help refresh links in existing category buyers and stave off decay.

Look for opportunities to include assets you want to build. The quality of every asset-building effort should be scrutinised to determine if it draws viewers' attention, and if that attention also includes the brand name.

Commandment 4: Resist change

Much of *Building Distinctive Brand Assets* has been about the importance of consistency. When assets have been embedded for a while, it is tempting to tinker with them. Don't. Changing your brand's identity is like inviting someone around for dinner, and then moving house without telling them, while still expecting your dinner guests to turn up at 7 p.m. on Thursday.

Treat every moment where the asset is present as a 'do or damage' moment. If you don't use the asset well it will decay but, if your brand's activities are inconsistent, you risk creating alternative memory pathways. Both of these reduce the chance of retrieval.

Fight the natural urge that will bubble up in you and others to change your Distinctive Assets. Assets don't need to have shelf lives, so don't ask consumers if they are tired of something—they are poor judges. Distinctive Asset obsolescence is only an outcome if planning is poor.

If you are tempted to refresh or update an asset, think of the logical outcomes:

- category buyers don't notice—in which case what is the point of the change
- category buyers do notice—and the change disturbs their recognition system, and your brand loses past investments (and sales)
- category buyers do notice and complain—this gets publicity and you are forced to change the brand back to show you are 'listening' to a small group of vocal customers.

It's easy to think a change will strengthen the brand, but do test any change carefully, particularly packaging assets. Set a high bar for what the change needs to achieve to undertake it: keeping the status quo is not sufficient justification for change. Some of the best Distinctive Asset projects I have been involved with actually resulted in no action being taken, whereby the client avoided changes that would have damaged the brand.

Following these four commandments will help you to make smart decisions, and importantly, protect the assets your efforts have built, so they will be around for the long term.

The Final Word

I finished the final draft of *Building Distinctive Brand Assets* in New York City and, given its topic, it seemed fitting to visit one of my favourite places to be visually stimulated: the Museum of Modern Art (MOMA). If nothing else, I thought I could write about such a visit and reassure readers that I was not a total philistine, and can appreciate great art and design. Indeed, rest assured I do appreciate beauty and aesthetics, but I also value the functional role of Distinctive Assets for a brand; this is what can increase sales. While beauty is in the (subjective) eye of the beholder, the functional role of Distinctive Assets is in the (more objective) brain. The brain is not perfect—it has its own fallibilities and challenges—but these are not trends and whims, so are much easier to work with to build a long-term strong brand identity.

It is hard to take off the mindset of an empirical generalist, whereby I see patterns everywhere. As I walked around MOMA appreciating the different exhibits, I was struck how artists suffer the same challenge as brands: standing out in a crowded environment. Indeed there were pieces of art that were surrounded with viewers, and many other examples, even by the same artist, that people largely passed by.

At a distance I could spot the well-known styles of Van Gogh, Picasso, Pollock and Monet. I could also easily find my personal favourites such as Miró and Duchamp, recognising the unique styles of these 'smaller brand' artists who had made it into my personal repertoire but did not seem to attract the interest of the masses. There were also many pieces of art I gave cursory, if any, attention, a pattern that seemed to mirror the behaviour of the people around me. Different people stopped at different pieces, but some pieces were more popular for everyone.

I also visited the Frank Lloyd Wright exhibition and was struck by the level of detail he went into to ensure every part of a design fitted together, from the structure to the fittings to the furniture. This consistency across all components helps the Frank Lloyd Wright style be identified and endure, as evidenced by the chairs, windows and furnishing examples that accompanied the sketches of his many buildings.

I don't claim to have the ingredients to make an artist successful, but having a distinctive style that enabled a piece to be easily found in a crowd seemed to help in gaining the attention of MOMA's patrons. And I imagine such traffic is monitored by museum buyers when deciding on which artists to stock. Perhaps art and product design are not that different after all.

I look forward to your feedback on *Building Distinctive Brand Assets* and how these ideas have helped you build the strong Distinctive Assets your brands deserve. You can connect with me on LinkedIn or reach me via email at jenni@marketingscience.info.

Jenni

REFERENCES

AJ 2015, '10 of the highest paid celebrity endorsement deals', *The Richest*, 2 February, <http://www.therichest.com/expensive-lifestyle/money/10-of-the-highest-paid-celebrity-endorsement-deals/>.

Alba, JW & Chattopadhyay, A 1986, 'Salience effects in brand recall', *Journal of Marketing Research*, vol. 23, pp. 363–9.

Anderson, J & Reder, L 1999, 'The fan effect: New results and new theories', *Journal of Experimental Psychology: General*, vol. 128, pp. 186–97.

Anderson, JR 1983, 'A spreading activation theory of memory', *Journal of Verbal Learning and Verbal Behavior*, vol. 22, pp. 261–95.

Anderson, JR & Bower, GH 1979, *Human Associative Memory*, Lawrence Erlbaum, Hillsdale, NJ.

Andrews, R 2009 'Confirmed: Compare the meerkat was devised by "drunk" ad men', *Gigaom*, 4 September, <https://gigaom.com/2009/09/04/419-confirmed-compare-the-meerkat-was-devised-by-drunk-ad-men/>.

Anesbury, Z, Nenycz Thiel, M, Dawes, J & Kennedy, R 2016, 'How do shoppers behave online? An observational study of online grocery shopping', *Journal of Consumer Behaviour*, vol. 15, pp. 261–70.

Barnard, NR & Ehrenberg, A 1990, 'Robust measures of consumer brand beliefs', *Journal of Marketing Research*, vol. 27, pp. 477–84.

Beard, F. 2013, 'Practitioner views of comparative advertising: How practices have changed in two decades', *Journal of Advertising Research*, vol. 53, pp. 313–23.

Beizer, J & Zack, A 2017, 'Behind HuffPost's new logo and look', *HuffPost*, 25 April, <http://www.huffingtonpost.com/entry/huffpost-new-logo-design_us_58fe7104e4b018a9ce5ddd30>.

Bergkvist, L & Zhou, KQ 2016, 'Celebrity endorsements: A literature review and research agenda', *International Journal of Advertising*, vol. 35, pp. 642–63.

Bernard, BJ & Gage, NM 2007, *Cognition, Brain, and Consciousness*, Academic Press, Elsevier, London, UK.

Binet, L, Müllensiefen, D & Edwards, P 2013, 'The power of music', *Admap*, October, WARC.

Brickman, P, Coates, D & Janoff-Bulman, R 1978, 'Lottery winners and accident victims: Is happiness relative?', *Journal of Personality and Social Psychology*, vol. 36, pp. 917–27.

Calder, S 2016, 'La Compagnie: The business-class transatlantic airline closes its London–New York route', *Independent*, 5 September, <http://www.independent.co.uk/travel/news-and-advice/america-holidays-new-york-london-business-class-flights-la-compagnie-route-closes-a7226911.html>.

Caruso, W, Bogomolova, S, Corsi, A, Cohen, J, Sharp, A & Lockshin, L 2015, 'Exploring the effectiveness of endcap locations in a supermarket: Early evidence from instore video observations', Australia and New Zealand Marketing Academy (ANZMAC) conference, 30 November, University of New South Wales, Sydney, Australia.

Chou, HY & Lien, NH 2010, 'Advertising effects of songs' nostalgia and lyrics' relevance', *Asia Pacific Journal of Marketing and Logistics*, vol. 22, pp. 314–29.

Collins, AM & Loftus, EF 1975, 'A spreading activation theory of semantic processing', *Psychological Review*, vol. 82, pp. 407–28.

Coté, J 2007, 'Robbers relish iPod craze/Little white earbuds are almost everywhere, particularly on BART—thieves are capitalizing on players' popularity', *SFGate*, 21 March, <http://www.sfgate.com/crime/article/Robbers-relish-iPod-craze-Little-white-earbuds-2607983.php>.

Craik, FIM & Watkins, MJ 1973, 'The role of rehearsal in short-term memory', *Journal of Verbal Learning and Verbal Behavior*, vol. 12, pp. 599–607.

Dahlén, M & Rosengren, S 2005, 'Brands affect slogans affect brands? Competitive interference, brand equity and the brand–slogan link', *Brand Management*, vol. 12, pp. 151–64.

Danenberg, N, Kennedy, R, Beal, V & Sharp, B 2016, 'Advertising budgeting: A re-investigation of the evidence on brand size and spend', *Journal of Advertising*, vol. 45, pp. 139–46.

Dass, M, Kohli, C. Kumar, P & Thomas, S 2014, 'A study of the antecedents of slogan liking', *Journal of Business Research*, vol. 67, pp. 2504–11.

Davies, M n.d., *Word and phrase: info* <http://www.wordandphrase.info/frequencyList.asp>.

Dawes, J & Nenycz-Thiel, M 2014, 'Comparing retailer purchase patterns and brand metrics for in-store and online grocery purchasing', *Journal of Marketing Management*, vol. 30, pp. 364–82.

Desai, KK & Hoyer, WD 2000, 'Descriptive characteristics of memory-based consideration sets: Influence of usage occasion frequency and usage location frequency', *Journal of Consumer Research*, vol. 27, pp. 309–23.

Dickson, PR & Sawyer, AG 1990, 'The price knowledge and search of supermarket shoppers', *Journal of Marketing*, vol. 54, pp. 42–53.

d0nkeyshines 2011, 'Arnott's Yo-Yo biscuits', *YouTube*, 2 April, <https://www.youtube.com/watch?v=IsbHrhmm66I>.

Ehrenberg, A, Barnard, N, Kennedy, R & Bloom, H 2002, 'Brand advertising as creative publicity', *Journal of Advertising Research*, vol. 42, pp. 7–18.

Erfgen, C, Zenker, S & Sattler, H 2015, 'The vampire effect: When do celebrity endorsers harm brand recall?', *International Journal of Research in Marketing*, vol. 32, pp. 155–63.

Express Web Desk 2017, 'Virat Kohli charges more than other cricketers, Bollywood celebrities in brand endorsement', *Revenge News*, 2 April, <http://www.revengenews.com/virat-kohli-charges-more-than-other-cricketers-bollywood-celebrities-in-brand-endorsement/>.

Fajardo, TM, Zhang, J & Tsiros, M 2016, 'The contingent nature of the symbolic associations of visual design elements: The case of brand logo frames', *Journal of Consumer Research*, vol. 43, pp. 549–66.

Fisher, K 2017, 'Katy Perry becomes first person to reach 100 million Twitter followers', *ENews*, 17 June, <http://www.eonline.com/news/861515/katy-perry-becomes-first-person-to-reach-100-million-twitter-followers>.

Gaillard, E, Sharp, A & Romaniuk, J 2006, 'Measuring brand distinctive elements in an in-store packaged goods consumer context', European Marketing Academy Conference (EMAC), 23–26 May, Athens Business and Economics University, Athens, Greece.

Gobbini, MI, Gors, JD, Halchenko, YO, Rogers, C, Guntupalli, JS, Hughes, H & Cipolli, C 2013, 'Prioritized detection of personally familiar faces', *PLoS One*, vol. 8, pp. 1–7.

Groeppel-Klein, A 2014, 'Success with pleasure: Interview with Helmut Meysenburg, BMW', *GfK Insights* blog, 11 June, <https://blog.gfk.com/2014/06/success-with-pleasure-interview-with-helmut-meysenburg-bmw/>.

Haley, RI & Baldinger, AL 2000, 'The ARF copy research validity project', *Journal of Advertising Research*, December/January, pp. 114–35.

Harrison, F 2013, 'Digging deeper down into the empirical generalization of brand recall', *Journal of Advertising Research*, vol. 53, pp. 181–85.

Hartnett, N 2011, 'Distinctive assets and advertising effectiveness', Master's thesis, University of South Australia, Adelaide.

Hartnett, N, Kennedy, R, Sharp, B & Greenacre, L 2016, 'Creative that sells: How advertising execution affects sales', *Journal of Advertising*, vol. 45, pp. 102–12.

Hartnett, N, Romaniuk, J & Kennedy, R 2016, 'Comparing direct and indirect branding in advertising', *Australasian Marketing Journal*, vol. 24, pp. 20–8.

Hasher, L & Zacks, RT 1984, 'Automatic processing of fundamental information: The case of frequency of occurrence', *American Psychologist*, vol. 39, pp. 1372–88.

Hilbert, M 2012, 'How to measure "how much information"? Theoretical, methodological, and statistical challenges for the social sciences', *International Journal of Communication*, vol. 6, no. 1, pp. 1042–55.

Hintzman, DL 1988, 'Judgments of frequency and recognition memory in a multiple-trace memory model', *Psychological Review*, vol. 95, pp. 528–51.

Hintzman, DL & Block, RA 1971, 'Repetition and memory: Evidence for a multiple-trace hypothesis', *Journal of Experimental Psychology*, vol. 88, pp. 297–306.

Holden, SJS 1993, 'Understanding brand awareness: Let me give you a c(l)ue!', *Advances in Consumer Research*, vol. 20, pp. 383–88.

Hoorens, V 1993, 'Self-enhancement and superiority biases in social comparison', *European Review of Social Psychology*, vol. 4, pp. 113–39.

Hoyer, WD 1984, 'An examination of consumer decision making for a common repeat purchase product', *Journal of Consumer Research*, vol. 11, pp. 822–9.

Janiszewski, C, Kuo, A & Tavassoli, NT 2013, 'The influence of selective attention and inattention to products on subsequent choice', *Journal of Consumer Research*, vol. 39, pp. 1258–74.

Jayasinghe, L & Ritson, M 2013, 'Everyday advertising context: An ethnography of advertising response in the family living room', *Journal of Consumer Research*, vol. 40, pp. 104–21.

Jones, JP 1990, 'Ad spending: Maintaining market share', *Harvard Business Review*, vol. 68, pp. 38–43.

Kanwisher, N, McDermott, J & Chun, MM 1997, 'The fusiform face area: A module in human extrastriate cortex specialized for face perception', *Journal of Neuroscience*, vol. 17, pp. 4302–11.

Kashmiri, M, Nguyen, C & Romaniuk, J 2017, 'Are two a crowd? Examining the prevalence of multi-brands on product packaging', Working paper, Ehrenberg-Bass Institute.

Keller, KL 1993, 'Conceptualizing, measuring, and managing customer-based brand equity', *Journal of Marketing*, vol. 57, pp. 1–22.

Kiley, D 2004, 'Can you name that slogan?', *Bloomberg*, 14 October, <http://www.businessweek.com/bwdaily/dnflash/oct2004/nf20041014_4965_db035.htm>.

Kitamura, T, Ogawa, SK, Roy, DS, Okuyama, T, Morrissey, MD, Smith, LM, Redondo, RL & Tonegawa, S 2017, 'Engrams and circuits crucial for systems consolidation of a memory', *Science*, vol. 356, pp. 73–8.

Klofstad, C., Anderson, RC & Peters, S 2012, 'Sounds like a winner: Voice pitch influences perception of leadership capacity in both men and women', *Proceedings of the Royal Society of London B: Biological Sciences*, vol. 279, pp. 2698–704.

Knoll, J & Matthes, J 2017, 'The effectiveness of celebrity endorsements: A meta-analysis', *Journal of the Academy of Marketing Science*, vol. 45, pp. 55–75.

Kohli, C, Leuthesser, L & Suri, R 2007, 'Got slogan? Guidelines for creating effective slogans', *Business Horizons*, vol. 50, pp. 415–22.

Kohli, C, Thomas, S & Suri, R 2013, 'Are you in good hands? Slogan recall: What really matters', *Journal of Advertising Research*, vol. 53, pp. 31–42.

Krader, K 2017, 'Restaurants put branding directly on their food to win Instagram', *Bloomberg*, 8 June, <https://www.bloomberg.com/news/articles/2017-06-08/restaurants-are-branding-burgers-ramen-cocktails>.

La Monica, PR 2016, 'Good grief! MetLife is dumping Snoopy', *CNN Money*, 20 October, <http://money.cnn.com/2016/10/20/investing/metlife-snoopy-peanuts-blimp/index.html>.

Lang, C 2016, 'This is the world's ugliest color—and it has an important job', *Time*, 2 June, <http://time.com/4353765/worlds-ugliest-color-discourages-smoking/>.

Larson, JS, Bradlow, ET & Fader, PS 2005, 'An exploratory look at supermarket shopping paths', *International Journal of Research in Marketing*, vol. 22, pp. 395–414.

Le Boutillier, J, Le Boutillier, SS & Neslin, SA 1994, 'A replication and extension of the Dickson and Sawyer price-awareness study', *Marketing Letters*, vol. 5, pp. 31–42.

Lopez, G 2015, 'John Oliver wants "Jeff the Diseased Lung" to become the face of tobacco companies', *Vox*, 16 February, <http://www.vox.com/2015/2/16/8045745/john-oliver-tobacco>.

Major, J, Romaniuk, J & Nenycz-Thiel, M 2012, 'The sound of music versus the rock of ages: Music in advertising', Australia and New Zealand Marketing Academy (ANZMAC) conference, 3 December, University of South Australia, Adelaide.

Matsuo, A 2014, '7 Richest commercial actors', *The Richest*, 21 February, <http://www.therichest.com/rich-list/world/5-richest-commercial-actors>.

McAlone, N 2017, 'These are the 18 most popular YouTube stars in the world—and some are making millions', *Business Insider*, 7 March, <http://www.businessinsider.com/most-popular-youtuber-stars-salaries-2017/#no-1-pewdiepie-541-million-subscribers-18>.

McClelland, JL & Chappell, M 1998, 'Familiarity breeds differentiation: A subjective-likelihood approach to the effects of experience in recognition memory', *Psychological Review*, vol. 105, pp. 724–60.

McCracken, G 1989, 'Who is the celebrity endorser? Cultural foundations of the endorsement process', *Journal of Consumer Research*, vol. 16, pp. 310–21.

Meyers-Levy, J 1989, 'The influence of a brand name's association set size and word frequency on brand memory', *Journal of Consumer Research*, vol. 16, pp. 197–207.

Miller, DW & Toman, M 2016, 'An analysis of rhetorical figures and other linguistic devices in corporation brand slogans', *Journal of Marketing Communications*, vol. 22, pp. 474–93.

Mocanu, A 2015, 'The prototypicality of consumer packaged goods: An atomistic versus holistic assessment of packaging design', PhD thesis, University of South Australia, Adelaide.

Mortein 2015, 'Louie the Fly', <http://www.mortein.com.au/about/about-louie>.

Neeley, SM & Schumann, DW 2004, 'Using animated spokes-characters in advertising to young children: Does increasing attention to advertising lead to product performance?', *Journal of Advertising*, vol. 33, pp. 7–23.

Nelson-Field, K 2013, *Viral Marketing: The Science of Sharing*, Oxford University Press, Melbourne.

Nelson-Field, K & Romaniuk, J 2013, 'Brand prominence and sharing', in Nelson-Field, K (ed.) *Viral Marketing: The Science of Sharing*, pp. 43–56, Oxford University Press, Melbourne.

Nenycz-Thiel, M & Romaniuk, J 2011, 'The nature and incidence of private label rejection', *Australasian Marketing Journal*, vol. 19, pp. 93–9.

Nenycz-Thiel, M & Romaniuk, J 2016, 'Online shopping . . . Is it different?', in Romaniuk, J & Sharp, B (eds.), *How Brands Grow: Part 2*, pp. 173–86, Oxford University Press, Melbourne.

Nenycz-Thiel, M, Romaniuk, J & Sharp, B 2016, 'Building physical availability', in Romaniuk, J & Sharp, B (eds), *How Brands Grow: Part 2*, pp. 146–72, Oxford University Press, Melbourne

Newstead, K 2014, 'Branding element variation: A consumer and industry examination', Master's thesis, University of South Australia, Adelaide.

Nielsen 2016, 'Audio today: Radio 2016—appealing far and wide', *Nielsen*, 25 February, <http:www.nielsen.com/us/en/insights/reports/2016/audio-today-radio-2016-appealing-far-and-wide.html>.

Nogales, AF & Suarez, MG 2005, 'Shelf space management of private labels: A case study in Spanish retailing', *Journal of Retailing and Consumer Services*, vol. 12, pp. 205–16.

OfCom 2015, *International Communications Market Report 2015*, OfCom, London.

OffbeatFrontier 2010, 'Mac Tonight commercial', *YouTube*, 9 April, <https://www.youtube.com/watch?v=0c4_b5PHWg8>.

Ogilvy, D & Raphaelson, J 1982, 'Research on advertising techniques that work—and don't work', *Harvard Business Review*, July–August, pp. 14–18.

O'Reilly, L 2014, 'Pepsi's new green cola looks exactly like Coca-Cola's new green cola', *Business Insider Australia*, 2 October, <https://www.businessinsider.com.au/pepsi-has-launched-a-new-green-cola-pepsi-true-2014-10?r=US&IR=T>.

Padmore, N 2016, 'Specsavers trademark application highlights the power of using language as a logo', *Campaign*, 19 August, <http://www.campaignlive.co.uk/article/specsavers-trademark-application-highlights-power-using-language-logo/1406192>.

Paech, S, Riebe, E & Sharp, B 2003, 'What do people do in advertisement breaks?' Australia and New Zealand Marketing Academy (ANZMAC) conference, 1 December, University of South Australia, Adelaide.

Pieters, R & Wedel, M 2004, 'Attention capture and transfer in advertising: Brand, pictorial, and text-size effects', *Journal of Marketing*, vol. 68, pp. 36–50.

Piñero, MA, Lockshin, L, Kennedy, R & Corsi, A 2010, 'Distinctive elements in packaging (FMCG): An exploratory study', Australia and New Zealand Marketing Academy (ANZMAC) conference, 29 November, University of Canterbury, Christchurch, New Zealand.

Rojas-Mèndez, JI, Davies, G & Madran, C 2009, 'Universal differences in advertising avoidance behavior: A cross-cultural study', *Journal of Business Research*, vol. 62, pp. 947–54.

Romaniuk, J 2003, 'Brand attributes—"distribution outlets" in the mind', *Journal of Marketing Communications*, vol. 9, pp. 73–92.

Romaniuk, J 2009, 'The efficacy of brand-execution tactics in TV advertising, brand placements and Internet advertising', *Journal of Advertising Research*, vol. 49, pp. 143–50.

Romaniuk, J 2013, 'Sharing the spotlight: Is there room for two brands in one advertisement?', *Journal of Advertising Research*, vol. 53, pp. 247–50.

Romaniuk, J 2016a, 'Building mental availability', in Romaniuk, J & Sharp, B (eds), *How Brands Grow: Part 2*, pp. 62–86, Oxford University Press, Melbourne.

Romaniuk, J 2016b, 'Leveraging distinctive assets', in Romaniuk, J & Sharp, B (eds), *How Brands Grow: Part 2*, pp. 87–108, Oxford University Press, Melbourne.

Romaniuk, J 2016c, 'Achieving reach', in Romaniuk, J & Sharp, B (eds), *How Brands Grow: Part 2*, pp. 110–24, Oxford University Press, Melbourne.

Romaniuk, J, Beal, V & Uncles, M 2013, 'Achieving reach in a multi-media environment: How a marketer's first step provides the direction for the second', *Journal of Advertising Research*, vol. 53, pp. 221–30.

Romaniuk, J, Bogomolova, S & Dall'Olmo Riley, F 2012, 'Brand image and brand usage: Is a forty-year-old empirical generalization still useful?', *Journal of Advertising Research*, vol. 52, pp. 243–51.

Romaniuk, J & Nenycz-Thiel, M 2014, 'Measuring the strength of color brand-name links: The comparative efficacy of measurement approaches', *Journal of Advertising Research*, vol. 54, pp. 313–19.

Romaniuk, J & Nenycz-Thiel, M 2017, 'The impact of early branding on YouTube preroll advertising audience retention', Working paper, Ehrenberg-Bass Institute for Marketing Science, Adelaide.

Romaniuk, J, Nguyen, C & Simmonds, L 2017, 'The effectiveness of celebrities as a branding device', Working paper, Ehrenberg-Bass Institute for Marketing Science, Adelaide.

Romaniuk, J & Sharp, B 2003a, 'Brand salience and customer defection in subscription markets', *Journal of Marketing Management*, vol. 19, pp. 25–44.

Romaniuk, J & Sharp, B 2003b, 'Measuring brand perceptions: Testing quantity and quality', *Journal of Targeting, Measurement and Analysis for Marketing*, vol. 11, pp. 218–29.

Romaniuk, J & Sharp, B 2004, 'Conceptualizing and measuring brand salience', *Marketing Theory*, vol. 4, pp. 327–42.

Rosch, E & Mervis, CB 1975, 'Family resemblances: Studies in the internal structure of categories', *Cognitive Psychology*, vol. 7, pp. 573–605.

Ryan, T 2015, 'The story of the Coca-Cola bottle', *Coca-Cola Journey*, 26 February, <http://www.coca-colacompany.com/stories/the-story-of-the-coca-cola-bottle>.

Sacktor, TC 2014, 'Long-term memory is immutable', *2014: What Scientific Idea is Ready for Retirement?*, Edge, <https://www.edge.org/response-detail/25537>.

Sharp, B 2010a, *How Brands Grow*, Oxford University Press, Melbourne.

Sharp, B 2010b, 'How brands grow', in Sharp, B (ed.), *How Brands Grow*, pp. 16–27, Oxford University Press, Melbourne.

Sharp, B, Riebe, E & Nelson-Field, K 2013, 'Media decisions: Reaching buyers with advertising', in Sharp, B. (ed.) *Marketing: Theory, Evidence, Practice*, pp. 378–437, Oxford University Press, Melbourne.

Sharp, B & Romaniuk, J 2010, 'Differentiation versus distinctiveness', in Sharp, B (ed.), *How Brands Grow*, pp. 112–33, Oxford University Press, Melbourne.

Sharp, B, Wright, M & Goodhardt, G 2002, 'Purchase loyalty is polarised into either repertoire or subscription patterns', *Australasian Marketing Journal*, vol. 10, pp. 7–20.

Slattery, L 2017, 'Bulmers calls time on long-running advertising theme', *The Irish Times*, 16 March, <http://www.irishtimes.com/business/media-and-marketing/bulmers-calls-time-on-long-running-advertising-theme-1.3011964>.

Smit, EG, Boerman, SC & Van Meurs, L 2015, 'The power of direct context as revealed by eye tracking: A model tracks relative attention to competing editorial and promotional content', *Journal of Advertising Research*, vol. 55, pp. 216–27.

Soniak, M 2012, 'Which came first: Orange the colour or orange the fruit?', *Mental Floss*, 8 February, <http://mentalfloss.com/article/29942/which-came-first-orange-color-or-orange-fruit>.

Sorensen, H, Bogomolova, S, Anderson, K, Trinh, G, Sharp, A, Kennedy, R, Page, B & Wright, M 2017, 'Fundamental patterns of in-store shopper behavior', *Journal of Retailing and Consumer Services*, vol. 37, pp. 182–94.

Steinbuch, Y 2015, 'Jared Fogle pleads guilty, blames diet for his sex crimes', *New York Post*, 19 November, <http://nypost.com/2015/11/19/subways-jared-pleads-guilty-to-kiddie-porn-and-sex-crime-charges>.

Stewart, DW & Furse, DH 1986, *Effective Television Advertising: A Study of 1000 Commercials*, Lexington Books, Lexington, MA.

Stewart, DW & Koslow, S 1989, 'Executional factors and advertising effectiveness: A replication', *Journal of Advertising*, vol. 18, pp. 21–32.

Svenson, O 1981, 'Are we all less risky and more skillful than our fellow drivers?' *Acta Psychologica*, vol. 47, pp. 143–8.

Taube, A 2017, 'The 21 best Absolut Vodka print ads of all time', *Business Insider Australia*, 29 December, <https://www.businessinsider.com.au/the-21-best-absolut-ads-2013-12?r=US&IR=T#21-absolut-24th-1>.

Taylor, CR 2015, 'The imminent return of the advertising jingle', *International Journal of Advertising*, vol. 34, pp. 717–19.

Telegraph 2012, 'Students get cute at the world's only mascot school in Japan', *The Telegraph* (UK), 21 November, <http://www.telegraph.co.uk/news/newstopics/howaboutthat/9693740/Students-get-cute-at-the-worlds-only-mascot-school-in-Japan.html>.

Tilley, J 2017, 'Orangina strips off for the summer', *AsianTrader*, 6 April, <https://www.asiantrader.biz/orangina-strips-off-for-the-summer/>.

Tulving, E 1972, 'Episodic and semantic memory', in *Organization of Memory*, pp. 381–402, Oxford University Press, New York.

Tulving, E & Craik, FIM 2000, *The Oxford Handbook of Memory*, Oxford University Press, Oxford.

Vaughan, K, Beal, V & Romaniuk, J 2016, 'Can brand users really remember advertising more than nonusers? Testing an empirical generalization across six advertising awareness measures', *Journal of Advertising Research*, vol. 56, pp. 311–20.

Walker, D & Von Gonten, MF 1989, 'Explaining related recall outcomes: New answers from a better model', *Journal of Advertising Research*, vol. 29, pp. 11–21.

Ward, E. 2017, 'Is sharing really caring? A descriptive investigation of brand sharing for distinctive asset types', Master's thesis, University of South Australia, Adelaide.

Wedel, M & Pieters, R 2006, 'Eye tracking for visual marketing', *Foundations and Trends® in Marketing*, vol. 1, pp. 231–320.

Winchester, M & Romaniuk, J 2008, 'Negative brand beliefs and brand usage', *International Journal of Market Research*, vol. 50, pp. 355–75.

Winchester, M, Romaniuk, J & Bogomolova, S 2008, 'Positive and negative brand beliefs and brand defection/uptake', *European Journal of Marketing*, vol. 42, pp. 553–70.

Winocur, G, Moscovitch, M & Bontempi, B 2010. 'Memory formation and long-term retention in humans and animals: Convergence towards a transformation account of hippocampal–neocortical interactions', *Neuropsychologia*, vol. 48, pp. 2339–56.

Zajonc, RB 1968, 'Attitudinal effects of mere exposure', *Journal of Personality and Social Psychology*, vol. 9, no. 2, part 2, pp. 1–26.

Zmunda, N 2009, 'Tropicana line's sales plunge 20% post-rebranding', *AdAge*, 2 April <http://adage.com/article/news/tropicana-line-s-sales-plunge-20-post-rebranding/135735/>.